The
Central
Thought
of
God

Witness Lee

Living Stream Ministry
Anaheim, California

First Edition, November 1998.

ISBN 0-7363-0424-X

Published by

Living Stream Ministry
2431 W. La Palma Ave., Anaheim, CA 92801 U.S.A.
P. O. Box 2121, Anaheim, CA 92814 U.S.A.

Printed in the United States of America

98   99   00   01   02   03   /   9   8   7   6   5   4   3   2   1

CONTENTS

PREFACE

This book is composed of messages given by Brother Witness Lee in Los Angeles, California in the summer of 1963. Not all of the messages were reviewed by the speaker.

CHAPTER ONE

CHRIST AS LIFE
IN THE SEVEN DAYS OF CREATION

Scripture Reading: Gen. 1

THE CENTRAL THOUGHT OF GOD

Christ, the expression of God, and the church constitute the central thought of God. The central thought of God in this universe and in eternity is to have Christ as His expression through the church. If you apply this thought and realization to all the Scriptures you read, the Scriptures will be opened to you. You will have the insight to understand the Word of God. Without this kind of realization concerning the central thought of God, it is hard for anyone to understand the holy Bible, the divine record of God's thought. If you desire to know the real meaning of the divine Word, you have to know the central thought of this Word, which is Christ as the expression of God through the church. The entire Bible is full of this thought.

The apostle Paul told us that Christ and the church are the great mystery (Eph. 5:32). Christ as the expression of God and the church as the Body of Christ constitute the central thought of God. This is the greatest mystery in the whole universe. If you do not understand this mystery, you do not know the meaning of the universe and the meaning of your human life.

If we want to understand the thought, the meaning, of any book, we have to realize what it speaks of at the beginning and at the conclusion. It is exactly the same with the Bible. In this divine book, at the very beginning, there are two chapters revealing to us the principles and the outline with the main points of God's eternal purpose. In the very beginning of the holy Scriptures, in the first two chapters of Genesis, we have the outline of God's central thought, the blueprint of God's plan.

At the end of this divine book are the last two chapters, chapters twenty-one and twenty-two of the book of Revelation. In those two chapters we can see a picture of the consummation of God's plan, a picture of the issue of what God has been doing through all the generations, and a picture of the realization of the central thought of God. We must carefully consider these four chapters—the first two chapters of Genesis at the beginning of the Bible and the last two chapters of Revelation at the end of the Bible.

First, we need to see Christ as the expression of God and the church as the Body of Christ in the first chapter of the Bible. Christ is everywhere and Christ is everything in the Scriptures. Christ can be seen in every day of the six days of creation. In the first chapter of Genesis we can also see the church and the believers, the saints. Genesis 1 reveals Christ as the expression of God and us as the members of the Lord's Body, which is the church. The record of the divine thought in Genesis 1 and 2 was written in a figurative way. We have to see this record figuratively to get the right meaning.

THE SIGNIFICANCE OF THE SIX DAYS OF GOD'S WORK

Now let us consider the six days of God's work. God's work on the first day was, on the one hand, to send His Spirit to move upon, to brood over, the surface of the waters and, on the other hand, to call the light to shine (Gen. 1:2-3). Thus, on the first day were the brooding Spirit and the shining light. With this brooding and shining came the separation of light from darkness (vv. 4-5). Before this, there was no light, so there was no division, no separation, between light and darkness. Please remember that with the work of the first day there were the Spirit and the light. The light separates. Where light is, there is the discernment, the separation, the division.

On the second day God made the firmament, the expanse (vv. 6-8). The expanse is space. God created the expanse to divide the waters under it from the waters above it. On the second day, the expanse was the dividing element.

The work of the third day was to recover the land (vv. 9-13). The land had been created already but was buried by the deep waters. God brought the land out of the waters of death and caused the land to produce all kinds of life—the grass, the herbs, the trees, and so on.

On the fourth day, there was the recovery of all the light bearers, the sun, the moon, and the stars (vv. 14-19). There was the sun in the daytime and the moon and stars in the nighttime. On the fifth day, the living creatures in the waters were created. Then the flying creatures in the air were created (vv. 20-23).

On the sixth day the living creatures on the land—the cattle, the beasts, and creeping things—were created (vv. 24-25). Then man was created (vv. 26-27).

Now we need to see what these figures signify and reveal to us. At the beginning of Genesis 1 are the Spirit of God and the light, and at the end is man with the image and authority of God. In between are the dividing between light and darkness, the dividing between the waters above and the waters underneath, and the dividing between the land and the waters. Without these dividings, it is impossible to have any kind of life. After all these dividings, the land emerged to produce different kinds of life and to become a place to live for the living creatures.

On the first day there was no life but there was light. Life always follows light. It is not life that comes first, but light. On the first day was the Spirit with the light. On the second day were the divisions. Then on the third day was the producing of life. On the fourth day there were the bigger and more solid lights, the embodied lights; so after this there was more life. On the fifth day was the animal life, the life in the waters and the life in the air. On the sixth day was the life on the land. Eventually, there was the highest life of the creatures, which was the human life, a life with the image and authority of God, a life that could express God and represent God. The image of God is the expression of God, and the authority of

God is the representation of God. If you have the authority of God, you are the representative of God.

Now we can see that the direction of God's creation is toward life, and the goal of God's creation is life. Scientists spend much time studying the universe, and others try to study the first chapters of the Bible with scientific knowledge. They think that the story of creation in the Bible is unbelievable and untrustworthy. However, we have to know that this Bible is a book of life. God did not give us a record of the whole process concerning His creation. He gave us only a little bit to show us what His central thought is.

Similarly, the apostle John told us that, besides those things that were recorded in his Gospel, the Lord Jesus did many other things (John 21:25). The Lord did hundreds of miracles, yet the apostle John selected only a few and put them in his Gospel to prove and testify to us that Christ is the Son of God so that we may believe into Him and have life. This is the goal. This is the central thought of John.

God created the whole universe with myriads of things, yet He gave us a record of only two chapters concerning His creation. If He had given us the complete record of His creation, we would be overburdened. Actually, there is no need for us to know all these things. All these things are not God's goal or central thought. His goal, His central thought, is a life matter. The purpose of the record of the creation of the universe is to lead us to know life.

Genesis 1 tells us that on the third day life was produced. The third day is a day of life out of death, a day of resurrection. The Lord Christ Himself was the very life buried by the waters of death. It was on the third day that He was recovered from death to produce life. The Lord is typified by the land buried by the waters of death and recovered by the life power of God. He was brought out of death to produce life; we all were regenerated, reborn, by the resurrection of Christ (1 Pet. 1:3). When He was resurrected, we were raised up with Him from death (Eph. 2:6). We are like the plants produced out of the land. We are God's farm, God's cultivated land (1 Cor. 3:9b). By the resurrection of Christ, we were produced and made alive.

Someone wrote a hymn with the following lines: "There is sunshine in my soul today, / More glorious and bright / Than glows in any earthly sky, / For Jesus is my light" (*Hymns*, #343). After we are regenerated, we enjoy Christ as our light. After the third day, there were the sun, the moon, and the stars on the fourth day. After we have been regenerated, we have Christ as the sun shining within us to make us as the moon reflecting the light of the sun and to make us the shining stars. The fourth-day lights are the sun, the moon, and the stars. In the first chapter of Genesis the believers are typified by the stars (v. 16c). Daniel 12:3 says that those who turn many to righteousness shine like stars. In Revelation, the messengers of the churches, the spiritual ones who bear the responsibility of the testimony of Jesus, are the shining stars (1:16, 20; 2:1; 3:1). The church is typified by the moon in Genesis 1 (v. 16b), and Christ is typified by the sun, the greatest light bearer (v. 16a). Just as the moon is the reflection of the sun, so the church is the reflection of Christ. This typifies Christ with His Body, including all the members.

After this shining of Christ within us, we become like a fish or a bird. We can live in an environment which is impossible for others to live in. We can live in a situation of death. The water always kills, yet we can live and move in it. We are the "fish" because we have life. The water is salty, yet we are not salty. The water is full of death, full of sin, yet we are full of life, with nothing salty, nothing sinful. Moreover, sometimes we can fly in the air like the birds. We have the flying element in the divine life. Many times oppressions, trials, and temptations come to us, but we can declare to them, "All of these things are under my feet. There is no need for me to fight with you. I will fly above you." Following this, we have the more abundant life, a life that can work for God, that can do the will of God, that can move on this earth. Eventually, we have the life with the image of God to express God and the authority of God to represent God. This shows us that the goal, the direction, of God's record, which is also the central thought of God, is Christ and the church with the matter of life.

CHRIST IN GENESIS 1

Now let us consider what Christ is in the first chapter of Genesis. First, there is the Spirit of Christ. The Spirit of God in Genesis 1:2 is the Spirit of Christ, who is Christ Himself (Rom. 8:9-10). When the Spirit came, He brought the Word of God, and the Word of God is Christ Himself (John 1:1). Then there is the light. This is also Christ Himself (John 1:4; 8:12). The Spirit, the Word, and the light are all Christ Himself.

On the second day there was the firmament, the dividing element. This is the cross, the death of Christ. Where the cross is, there is always the dividing. At Calvary, on the day of the Lord's crucifixion, the cross was in the middle dividing the saved one from the perishing one (Luke 23:32-33, 39-43). Whenever we receive Christ and His cross, there is always a dividing element within us to divide the things above, the heavenly things, from the things underneath, the earthly things (Col. 3:1-3).

Then, as we have pointed out, on the third day was the land. The good land of Canaan is the all-inclusive type of Christ (Josh. 14:1; Col. 1:12). God's bringing the people of Israel into this land is a type of His saving us from the world and bringing us into Christ. Christ is the land in which we walk, that is, in which we live, act, behave, and have our being (Col. 2:6).

Christ is also typified by the trees. In Genesis 2:9 the tree of life is a type of Christ. In Exodus 15:23-25 we see another tree. One day, when the children of Israel came to Marah, they could not drink of the bitter waters there. Jehovah told Moses to cast a tree into the waters, and the waters were made sweet. That tree is also a type of Christ. In Song of Songs 2:3, the apple tree, which some think is a sort of orange tree, is also a type of Christ. Ezekiel 34:29 mentions "a plant of renown." This famous plant is Christ. Isaiah 11:1 says that "a twig will come forth from the stem of Jesse, / And a branch from his roots will bear fruit." Both the twig and the branch signify Christ. Then in John 15 the Lord told us that He is the vine tree (vv. 1, 5). Christ is the reality of the trees.

On the fourth day we see the sun as a type of Christ.

Christ is the Sun of righteousness (Mal. 4:2) with the church, His Body, as the moon reflecting His light and all His members as stars (cf. Gen. 37:9-11).

Then on the fifth day were the fish and the birds. Christ is typified by a bird. In Leviticus we are told that sometimes the burnt offerings had to be offered with turtledoves or young pigeons (1:14), which are types of Christ. Moreover, Christ is also signified by a fish. In John 6 the Lord fed five thousand people with five barley loaves and two fish (vv. 1-15). The barley loaves are of the vegetable life and signify Christ as the generating life. Fish are of the animal life and signify Christ as the redeeming life. Thus, the living creatures in the water also typify Christ.

On the sixth day were the beasts, the cattle, and the creeping things on the earth. Revelation 5:5 tells us that Christ is the Lion of the tribe of Judah. He is also the Lamb (John 1:29; 1 Pet. 1:19; Rev. 22:1, 3). The creeping things, with the serpent as the leading one, represent the enemy of Christ, but even Christ Himself came in the form of the serpent. John 3:14 says, "And as Moses lifted up the serpent in the wilderness, so must the Son of Man be lifted up." When Christ was crucified on the cross, He was in the form of the serpent but was without the serpent's poison.

Eventually, there was the man Adam. The first Adam was a figure of the last Adam, who is Christ (1 Cor. 15:45; Rom. 5:14). Moreover, Adam as the first man was a figure of Christ as the second man (1 Cor. 15:47).

This gives us a hint concerning how many items in Genesis 1 refer to Christ. The central thought of God is that Christ will be the expression of God through His church, shining all the time in life. Adam was a prefigure, a type, of Christ. Christ is the last Adam. Adam had the image of God (Gen. 1:26), and 2 Corinthians 4:4 says that Christ is the image of God. Christ as the image of God is the expression of God.

Furthermore, all authority in heaven and on earth has been given to Christ (Matt. 28:18). Genesis 1 is related to Psalm 8 and Hebrews 2. In Psalm 8 the psalmist referred to Genesis 1, and in Hebrews 2 the apostle spoke the same thing. The man in these portions of the Word points to Christ.

Christ is the very man with the image of God and with the authority of God. He expresses God and represents God. He is everything.

CHAPTER TWO

CHRIST AS THE EXPRESSION OF GOD

Scripture Reading: Gen. 1:26-28; Psa. 8:4-8; Heb. 2:6-9;
2 Cor. 4:4-6; Rom. 8:29; Eph. 4:24; Col. 3:10-11

THE MAIN ITEMS OF CREATION IN GENESIS 1

In the previous chapter we have seen the main items in
Genesis 1, the first chapter of the Scriptures. We have seen
that the direction of God's creation is toward the goal of life. ①
On the first day there was no life. There was only the Spirit of
God coming to shine, to move, to brood, and to bring light into
darkness. When the light came, there was the dividing. ⑪

On the third day there was the dividing of the land from
the waters. With the land there is life, and with the waters ⑨
there is death. With the land there are the riches of life ⑩
and the beauty of life. The third day is a symbol of the resur- ⑪
rection life. It is a day of resurrection. On the third day all the
different kinds of life—grass, herbs, trees—came into being.
All these kinds of life came into being on the land, through
the land, and from the land.

The land recovered from the burial of the waters of death ⑦
typifies Christ resurrected from death. He is the all-inclusive ②
land. With Him there are the riches of life. All the herbs, the ③
trees, the flowers, and the plants are figures of the riches of
Christ Himself as life. Christ is rich in life like all the plants.
Whenever you see a flower that is so beautiful and the trees
and grass that are so green, you have to realize that all these
things are signs, types, figures, of the very Christ of God. He ⑤
is rich in life. He is the One who was resurrected on the third ⑨
day. He is the One who was buried into the depths of death, ⑥
yet He was raised up. He was recovered. He was resurrected ⑥

from the dead to show that He is the Lord of life, the Author
of life (Acts 3:15). With Him there are the riches of life.

On the third day with the land we can also see the beauty
of life. The flowers reveal the beauty of Christ expressed in
His life. No one can exhaust speaking about the varieties of
flowers in their beauty. All these flowers are figures of the
beauties of Christ as life to us. This is something revealed
and taught by the Scriptures. Song of Songs 1:14 mentions
the henna flower, an Old-World plant with which Jewish girls
beautified themselves. Christ is a cluster of henna flowers.
He is beautiful. Not only so, in Song of Songs 1:13 Christ is
likened to a bundle of myrrh. Myrrh signifies the sweetness,
the sweet smell, of Christ. Christ is so sweet to us. Christ is
life to us in beauty and in sweetness.

In the second chapter of Song of Songs, Christ is likened to
an apple tree (v. 3). With Him there is the shadow under
which we are covered from the sunshine to enjoy rest, and
with Him there is the fruit which we can taste for our satisfaction. In the fifth chapter of Song of Songs, Christ is likened
to the cedars (v. 15). Cedars are big trees grown on the moun-
tains of Lebanon. They signify the greatness of Christ. The
plants—the trees, the grass, the flowers—are figures of
Christ as life to us. He is so beautiful, so sweet, so great, and
so rich!

We are told that most of these plants produced from the
land on the third day were the plants yielding fruit. This
means that they yield food for the life supply. Revelation 22:2
says that the tree of life produces twelve fruits, yielding its
fruit each month. Christ as life to us is not only beautiful,
sweet, and rich, but also supplying what we need all the time.
Thus, we can see that the land recovered on the third day is
an all-inclusive type of Christ, and all the plants produced
from the land represent the different aspects of Christ as life
to us.

On the fourth day were the greater lights, the embodied
lights. This means that there was more light and thus more
life would be produced. So on the fifth day we see the stronger
life in its riches and beauties. This is a life that can live in

salty water, that is, in an environment of death. This is another aspect of Christ being life to us.

In the sight of God, human society today is like a sea of death, a dead sea. Some American friends once asked me if I appreciated Los Angeles. I said, "Yes, I do, but you have to realize what Los Angeles is in the eyes of God. It is nothing but a dead sea, a sea full of death." Not only a big city but even a small village is a small part of the dead sea. However, Christ can live in this environment of death. If you have Christ as life, you can live in this dead sea. You can live in this salty water yet not be salted, not be affected or influenced by death.

When I first went to Shanghai, the biggest city in China, some people took me to the main street of the city and said, "Brother Lee, look at all these attractive and sinful stores. Are you not afraid that you will be affected?" I said, "Brothers, as far as myself is concerned, I am afraid. But as far as Christ is concerned, I am not afraid, because Christ is living within me all the time. He can live in the environment of death, yet He cannot be affected. He can never be influenced by anything of death." This is just like the fish. They can live in the salty water, but they can never be salted unless they are killed.

On the fifth day there was also a life that can fly. It is a life that is transcendent, a life that is above all. Nothing can suppress it, nothing can retain it, and nothing can hold it. This signifies Christ as life to us.

On the sixth day God created the cattle and the beasts of the earth. This is the life that can do something for man. The life of a dog is much stronger than that of a fish. Then there is the highest life among the creatures, which is the human life. This is a life that not only can live in death, be transcendent, work for God, and do the will of God, but also can express and represent God. This is a life with the image of God and the authority of God. It is at this point that God rested.

The completion of God's work is a life with His image and His authority. We may have thought that God rested because He had finished His work. But as long as there is not a life with the image and authority of God, there is no rest for God.

God is still working today in the New Testament age because there is the lack of such a life that is full of His image and His authority. The goal, the aim, of the Lord's work is to gain a life that can express Him and represent Him in a full way. If there is such a life, there is the completion of the work of God and God can have the rest, the Sabbath.

We need to see the picture of God's creation. It starts with the things without life, the inanimate things. Then gradually it goes on to different stages of life. First, it is the vegetable life, which is the lower life, a life without consciousness. Then it goes on to the higher life with a low consciousness. This includes the life of the fish, the birds, and even the cattle, the beasts, and the creeping things. Eventually, there is the highest life of the creatures with the highest consciousness. That is the human life, a life which can express and represent God. The central thought of God is to bring life to us so that we can bear His image and have His authority.

CHRIST IN GENESIS 1

We have also seen Christ typified in Genesis 1. On the first day are the Spirit of Christ, Christ as the word, and Christ as the light. On the second day is the cross of Christ. On the third day is the all-inclusive Christ as the land with all the riches and beauties of life. On the fourth day is Christ as the sun with the moon, including all the stars as a corporate, collective reflector of Christ. On the fifth day is the stronger life for the expression of Christ, and on the sixth day is an even stronger aspect of Christ as life. Eventually, there is a man as the all-inclusive figure of Christ. Christ as a man is the last Adam (1 Cor. 15:45).

Adam was created in the image of God. God is invisible, yet He has an image. His image is Christ Himself (Col. 1:15; 2 Cor. 4:4). Thus, Adam was created according to Christ. Adam was copied according to Christ, so he was a copy of Christ. The image of God is the expression of God. Christ as the image of God is the declaration, the expression, of God. He declares God and expresses God (John 1:18). Because Adam was created according to Christ and is a copy of Christ, we may say that he was the duplication and multiplication of Christ.

As the descendants of Adam, we are duplicates of Christ because we were made in the image of God. This means that we were made according to Christ in the expression of God. We are the copies, the duplication, the multiplication, of Christ. God created man because He had the intention to have Christ multiplied, increased, copied, duplicated. This is the very thought of God.

God's intention, God's desire, is to duplicate, to multiply, Christ, the expression of God. Christ was the only begotten Son of God from eternity, and in resurrection He became the Firstborn among many brothers (Rom. 8:29). He was the very image of God, but now He is the first one of many images of God. After God's creation, there is the duplication, the multiplication, of Christ. God created man, and that man is Christ in image and likeness.

Psalm 8 and Hebrews 2:6-9 show that the man referred to in Genesis 1 is Christ. Christ is a man. God is mindful of man and remembers man because man is the figure of Christ and the multiplication of Christ. God remembers nothing but Christ. God remembers you because you are the image, the expression, of Christ. God is mindful of you because you are one aspect of Christ, a duplicate of Christ, a copy of Christ. God remembers you not because of yourself but because of Christ. If you have nothing to do with Christ, God has no interest in you and will discard you. But God has a lot of interest in you because of Christ. The first time the Bible mentions something about man is in Genesis 1:26-28. Later on, in Hebrews 2:6-9, we are told that the man mentioned in Genesis 1 is Christ Himself. This is something mysterious. We have to see the central thought of God; then we will know what man is.

Man as a duplicate and figure of Christ was committed with the authority of God. God is the Head with the headship, but God committed His headship to this very man. He put everything under the control of this man, and this man in figure is Christ, who is the expression of God and the authority of God, the representative of God.

Why do we Christians have to realize the order of God's headship? Simply because we know something about man. Man is the duplicate and multiplication of Christ. With Christ, there is the authority of God, so we are under authority and have the order of authority. If you are not under authority, you can never exercise authority. If you are going to be the authority, you have to be under authority. If you can subject yourself to the authority of God, you can exercise the authority of God. Christ is the expression of God and the representative of God with the full authority of God's headship.

At the time of Genesis 1 God did not gain the real man of His desire. When the church is brought into existence, the church with the Head, Christ, is that real man. Ephesians 4:24 and Colossians 3:10 tell us that the real man is the new man. The church as the new man is the real man created according to the image of God.

Adam was just a figure, not the real man. The real man is the church. Adam had the form of Christ, but he did not have the life of Christ. Adam was just a photograph of Christ, without the life of Christ. Today the church has not only the form, the appearance, of Christ but also Christ as the living One, as life. The church with Christ as life is the real man God is after.

The central thought of God is to have such a man with the appearance, the form, the life, and everything of Christ. This is the new man, the real man. The human race is a figure because it just has the form, the appearance, of Christ, not the life, the substance, and nature of Christ. But today we as the church have not only the appearance, the form, of Christ but also the life, the nature, and the substance of Christ. As a member of the new man, we can say that we are Christ in life and in nature.

Actually, we were created when Adam was. On the one hand, God created one man, but on the other hand, millions were included in that one man. Therefore, what God created was not just an individual man but a collective man, a corporate man, a man including millions of sons and daughters. The new man is the church with many persons as a corporate, collective Body. Thus, in His creation God created a corporate man, and in His redemption He created a new man, which is the church. The man created in God's creation was just a man in form. That was not the real man. But the man created in God's redemption is the real man, the church. The church as the real man not only has the form, the appearance, of Christ but also the life, the nature, and the substance of Christ.

Therefore, in Genesis 1 we have Christ as everything. We also have Christ as the image, the expression, and the definition of God. Then we have the church, the Body, as the corporate expression of Christ. This is the central thought of God.

Since the fall, man has had a wrong concept of always wanting to do something for God, to work for God, but we have to give up this thought. We have to be corrected and adjusted. We have to see that the central thought of God is not that we do something for God or that we work for God. Rather, the central thought of God with us is that He can make us a part of Christ and that He can work Christ into us.

In the old creation, we had only the form, the appearance, of Christ. We were the duplication, the multiplication, of Christ in form, in appearance. We had neither the life of Christ nor the reality of Christ. Now in regeneration, God works Christ into us as life and as reality. What God desires is to make us the very living image, duplication, multiplication, of Christ. We have to give up all thoughts of doing anything for God or working for God. Rather, we have to see that we have to be worked on by God. We are not the workmen of God but the workmanship of God (Eph. 2:10). We are in the hand of God to be worked on by God that we may be the expression, the image, of Christ both in form and in reality. Hence, we need to be stopped from all kinds of work, even Christian work. We have to be broken and emptied that we may be wrought with Christ by the Spirit. God's central thought is to have Christ as everything to us so that we, as the Body of Christ, can be the expression, the image, of Christ.

About twenty years ago, I was very busy with the Lord's work. I was working all the time, day and night. At a certain point, the Lord put a stop to my work. At that time, I was really troubled. I asked the Lord, "Lord, what is this? I worked for You day and night. Why did You stop me from working for You?" In the first month, I did not understand. The more I prayed, "Lord, deliver me from all the troubles," the more troubles came. Physically, I was very ill; mentally, I was very perplexed; and financially, I was put into a terrible condition. One day the Lord said to me, "Do you want to know why I brought you into such a circumstance and why these things are happening to you? It is simply because you worked too much and did too much. Your concept is to do all the time, but what you need is not to do but to be done away with. It is not a matter of your working for Me but a matter of your being worked on by Me. You have to stop. To work for Me is not My central thought. This is not My mind. My mind is to have you worked on by Me. What is the measure of Christ in you? How much has Christ been wrought into you?" On that day, I could do nothing but prostrate myself before the Lord and confess that I had only a small measure of the fullness of Christ.

May the Lord reveal to you that the central thought of God is to make you a part of Christ and to make Christ everything to you in a very practical and living way, not in the way of doctrine or knowledge. How much have you realized Christ as your life? How much do you have of the measure of Christ? Your thought is to work, to preach, to teach, to do something for the Lord. But you have to realize that the central thought of God is to have Christ wrought into you.

Today's Christianity has very little measure of Christ. There are a lot of activities, a great deal of work, and different kinds of movements, but there is only a small measure of Christ. This is not something of the mind of God. We have to realize that in God's creation, the direction, the goal, is Christ as life and everything to us that we may be wrought by God with Christ to be the very expression, duplication, and multiplication of Christ in form, appearance, life, and reality.

In His creation, God did not tell man to do anything. Man was created in the image of God and then committed by God with His divine authority. Man had a life with the image of God to express God and with the authority of God to represent God, not a life to do something or to work something for God. Many times when you meet some Christians, you have the sense that they are busy people working for God. They are diligent and faithful. But you do not sense the expression and the authority of God. On the other hand, with some saints, it seems that they are not so busy and not so diligent working for God, yet you sense the expression of God and the authority of God. You have the sense that God is with them. They are people full of the presence of God. Whenever you meet them, you sense the expression and the headship, the authority, of God. This is what God is after.

May the Lord be merciful to us that we may see the central thought of God, that is, to have Christ wrought into us that we may become a part of Christ for God to have Himself expressed in us and to have His authority exercised through us.

CHAPTER THREE

THE DIVINE LIFE
FOR THE BRIDE OF CHRIST

Scripture Reading: Gen. 2:4-25

THE LIFE THAT CAN BRING REST TO GOD

From the previous chapters we realize that the life of man, the highest life among the creatures, is a life with the image of God and with the authority of God, so this life can bring rest to God. This is because this life can subdue the earth and all things on this earth. To subdue all things is to bring them under the control of God, in subjection to God. This means that before this subduing there must have been something in this universe and on this earth that was against God and needed to be subdued.

Genesis 1:28 tells us that God charged man to subdue the earth, not the waters or the air. This is because on this earth there was the serpent, the head of the creeping things. In Genesis 3 the serpent spoiled the man whom God created. God's intention is to have man wrought with His image and entrusted with His authority to represent Him on this earth and to subdue the earth with all the enemies, the creeping things. This will bring the earth and all things on the earth into subjection to God to bring rest to God. Rest implies satisfaction. It is when God can rest and is satisfied that His work is completed. This is the central thought of God. What God is seeking after today is a life that can bring Him rest.

Are you satisfied with your Christian life and with your church life? If you are not satisfied, how can God be satisfied? It is only when you are living a life with the image of God to express God and with the authority of God to represent God and subdue the enemies of God that you have rest and God has rest with you. Then you are satisfied, and God is also satisfied. This is the center of the divine mind. It is not your work and doings. I am afraid that the more you work, the more you will lose your rest and satisfaction. The more you try to do good or do something for God, the more you will be dissatisfied. We are being called to realize the central thought of God. If we will give up ourselves to enjoy Christ as everything to us, we will have the proper church life. Then we will have rest and be satisfied. When we are satisfied, God is also satisfied.

GOD'S DESIRE FOR MAN TO RECEIVE HIM
AS HIS LIFE AND LIFE SUPPLY

After man was created, on the one hand, God rested, but on the other hand, God's work was not completed because man did not yet have the divine life. Up to that point, man had the form and the appearance of God but not the life and nature, the substance, of God. In Genesis 1 there are the created lives in different degrees, but in Genesis 2 there is the unique and highest life, the divine life, the uncreated life, signified by the tree of life. Adam was made as the highest life among the created lives, but he did not have the divine life at the time of creation. God's intention was that Adam would take God as his life. Without the divine life being accepted, received, realized, and experienced by man, man can never be the expression and representative of God.

Man was made as a vessel to contain God as life. The human life is the vessel, but the divine life, the life which is God Himself, is the real life, the life which is able to express God and to represent God to exercise the authority to subdue all the enemies of God. After the first chapter of Genesis until the end of the whole Scripture, the primary matter is that the man created by God must receive God as his divine life. Hence, immediately after man was created, God put man in front of the tree of life with the intention that man would receive the tree of life as his food, his life supply. The tree of life is a symbol of God being our life and life supply.

The Lord told us repeatedly in the Gospel of John that we have to believe into Him and receive Him that we may have the eternal life, the life which is God Himself (1:4, 12-13; 3:15-16, 36; 11:25; 14:6). The Lord's word here is related to Genesis 2 and Revelation 21 and 22. After man's creation, the first thing, the primary thing, for man to pay attention to is to receive God as his life.

The second thing is that we have to be transformed into the image of God day by day in, by, and with the life of God so that we can be the expression of God. God has no intention to ask us to do anything for Him. We should give up that concept. God's intention is for us to be vessels to contain Him. We should not be the doing or working Christians but the receiving Christians, the eating Christians, and the drinking Christians. We have to receive God, feed on God in Christ, and drink of Christ as the Spirit. We have to be filled with God. God can do everything, but He cannot be a vessel for Himself. He needs us to be His vessels. As His vessels we need to receive, enjoy, eat, and drink God in Christ and by the Spirit.

After God created man, He did not tell him how to behave. God did not tell man to do anything except to take care of his eating. We have to pay full attention to what we eat. If we eat rightly, we will be in God's intention. If we eat wrongly, we will be usurped by God's enemy. After Adam was created, God did not say, "Adam, you have to be patient, be humble, love others, and make sure that you love your wife." Neither did God tell Eve, "Eve, you have to be clear that as a wife, you have to be submissive to your husband." God did not give them any commandment concerning their outward behavior. He simply told them to be careful about what they ate.

We have to receive, to eat, of the tree of life, which is to take Christ in as our life and life supply. In the Gospel of John, the Lord told us to believe into Him (3:15-16; 14:12), to love Him (14:15, 21, 23), to abide in Him (15:4-7), to eat Him (6:51, 57), and to drink Him (4:14; 7:37). As long as we experience and enjoy Christ by feeding on Him, receiving Him, and drinking of Him, we will be a satisfaction and a rest to God. When we are satisfied, God is satisfied. When we are at rest, God is at rest.

In the first chapter of Genesis there are the created lives in different degrees, but in the second chapter there is the divine life as the unique life, which is God Himself to be received, realized, and experienced by the created man. In this chapter we are told that man was an earthen vessel made of clay, of dust. Second Corinthians 4:7 says, "We have this treasure in earthen vessels." God Himself is the treasure, and we are the earthen vessels. Romans 9 also says that we are vessels to contain God (vv. 21, 23).

We are living vessels, living souls, with a spirit as the organ to receive Christ. Our body is a vessel with a stomach as an organ by which we can contain, receive, and digest food. Similarly, we were made as a vessel to contain God with an organ to receive God. This organ is our spirit. Man was made out of the dust with a body as the outward vessel, with a living soul as the personality, and with a spirit as the organ to receive God. God put this man at the "divine table" with the intention that he would eat the tree of life to receive the divine life as his life and life supply. This is the central thought of God. Our spiritual hunger is a sign that we need more of God, that we have to receive God once more as our life supply. We have to exercise our spirit to contact God in Christ through the Spirit. We need to eat the fruit of the tree of life not just once, but all the time.

THE DIVINE LIFE AND THE WIFE

After being created, Adam was short of two things. First, he was short of the divine life within, and second, he was short of a wife, a counterpart, to match him without. Adam was created in a complete form, but he was not completed. He needed to be completed by receiving God and by having a wife. Thus, in Genesis 2, God revealed to us that man was created completely as a vessel. However, he still needed to be completed with the divine life and with a counterpart, a helpmate, a wife. Adam needed to receive God as life into him to be filled with God. Then eventually, he would have a bride (Gen. 2:18-23).

After we have received God in Christ as life to us, and after we have realized, experienced, enjoyed, and appropriated

God as life to us, what will come out eventually will be the bride of Christ. The last item of the whole Scripture is a bride (Rev. 21:2, 9; 22:17). The holy city, the New Jerusalem, is the bride of the Lamb as the wife, the counterpart, of Christ. John the Baptist told us that Christ is both the Lamb (John 1:29) and the Bridegroom who will marry the bride (3:29). Today Christ is preached mostly as the redeeming Lamb, but Christ as the Bridegroom is neglected. The goal of the redemption of Christ is to have a bride.

The last item of Genesis 2 is a bride, a counterpart. We need to receive Christ, experience Christ, and be filled with Christ. Then the ultimate issue, the outcome, of this experience is that we will be built up together as a corporate bride to match Christ. The more we enjoy, experience, and realize Christ, the more we will be built up together as a corporate bride to Christ.

Our nature was earthen, but after we receive Christ as life, we have Him as a precious and excellent treasure within us. Second Corinthians 4:6-7 shows that when God shines in our hearts, Christ as the treasure comes into us, the earthen vessels. This treasure is as precious as gold. In the Scriptures, gold is a type of the divine nature of God. Now we have something of gold within us as our nature. This occurred at the time of our regeneration. By regeneration we received God as our nature.

We need to look at the picture in Genesis 2 to receive a revelation of God's central thought. A man was created of dust, clay, and then he was placed before the tree of life. Beside the tree of life there was a river flowing, and in the flow of the river there was gold. Today if we receive Christ as our life, there will be a flow of the living water within us, and in this flow there is the nature of gold. In the flow of the river there were also bdellium (pearl), something that is bright, and onyx stone, which is precious. This means that after our regeneration, there will be transformation, conformation, and even glorification which will involve a metabolic change in our spirit, soul, and body. We were made as clay, but we will be transformed into gold, pearl, and precious stones. After we are regenerated, we have the divine nature as gold. Then the

Lord continues to transform us from the human form to the divine form, from clay to something as precious as gold, pearl, and onyx stone.

We can sense that some saints are precious, as the precious stone, and so bright, as the pearl. But on the contrary, we can sense that other brothers and sisters are opaque and even in darkness. We cannot sense anything precious or weighty within them. They are like a piece of very thin paper, not like a piece of heavy stone. With them everything is superficial. This is because they have not experienced much transformation by the divine life within them.

After regeneration we have to be transformed from the natural form into the glorious form, the form of the divine life. We need to be transformed into the image of Christ from glory to glory (2 Cor. 3:18). When we are transformed into the nature of gold, the nature of pearl, and the nature of the onyx stone, we will be precious material for the building up of the church as the Body, as the bride to Christ. First, we have to receive Christ; second, we have to be transformed by Christ, through Christ, and with Christ; and third, we have to be built up together as the Body, as a corporate bride to match Christ. This is the central thought of God. This is the center of God's mind.

Many say that they have received a vision from the Bible or some revelation from the Scriptures, but I would ask, "What kind of revelation have you received?" One day a brother came to me with great excitement. He told me, "Brother Lee, I saw a great light in my Bible study this morning. I am a quick person. I think quickly, speak quickly, and act quickly. Everything with me is quick. So today the Lord revealed to me that I have to be slow." This is not wrong, but this is not the central thought of God. You may say that you have seen some light about a certain truth or about certain gifts, but we need to see what God's desire is. The central thought of the divine mind is that we, as living vessels to contain God, have to receive God in Christ and through the Spirit as life and the life supply into us; that we have to be transformed into gold, pearl, and precious stones; and that we have to be built up together as a living Body, a corporate bride with the nature, form, appearance, and essence of Christ as a living counterpart to match Christ. We must be controlled and directed by this light. This light will cause us to drop many other things which are less important, valuable, and weighty.

The apostle Paul told us that we must build the church with gold, silver, and precious stones. Silver stands for the same thing as pearl. In Genesis 2 there are gold, pearl, and precious stones (vv. 11-12). In 1 Corinthians 3 there are gold, silver, and precious stones (v. 12). Then in Revelation 21 in the last item of the Scriptures, the holy city, the New Jerusalem, there are gold, pearl, and precious stones. The city proper and the street of the city are gold (vv. 18b, 21b). All the entrances, the twelve gates, are pearls (v. 21a), and the stones for the building up of the wall are precious stones (vv. 18-20). Thus, from the beginning to the end of the Scriptures there are three kinds of materials. These materials come into being through the flowing of the current of the divine life.

After we have been built up together with others in the very flow of the divine life, we will be a part of the counterpart of Christ. We will be living, functioning members of Christ. Then Christ will be satisfied with us and we will be satisfied with Christ. This is what the Lord is after today.

CHAPTER FOUR

THE CHURCH—
THE COUNTERPART OF CHRIST

Scripture Reading: Gen. 1:26-28; 2:18-24; Eph. 5:30-32; 2:15b-16a; 4:24; 1:22-23; 1 Cor. 12:12; John 3:29-30; Rev. 21:2, 9; 22:1-2

We have seen that man has the highest life in God's creation, a life with the image of God to express God and with the authority of God to represent God to subdue all the enemies of God. In this way man can bring satisfaction and rest to God. By the help of the New Testament, we can realize that the man created by God is a type, a figure, pointing to the real man, who is Christ (Rom. 5:14). The first Adam is a type, a figure, of the last Adam (1 Cor. 15:45b), who is the real Adam. He is the Son of God incarnated as a man by the name of Jesus Christ.

Most of the items of God's creation are also types, figures, of Christ. The heavens, the earth, the plants, and the living creatures are figures of Christ. Eventually, man, the last item of God's creation, is a figure of Christ. All the things created by God are not the real things. The real thing is Christ Himself. The real heaven, the real earth, and the real light are Christ. The real plant, the real beauty, and the real order are Christ. The real word is Christ; He is the Word. If you do not have Christ, all that you have is false. Christ is everything as reality to us.

THE CORPORATE CHRIST

We also have to realize that the man created by God was not an individual man. Adam was a corporate man, a collective man, a man including himself and all his descendants.

In the same principle, Christ is not only an individual man. Christ is a collective man, a corporate man, composed of Christ Himself and all the members of Christ. Therefore, 1 Corinthians 12:12 says, "For even as the body is one and has many members, yet all the members of the body, being many, are one body, so also is the Christ." Christ is not only the Head but also the Body. This means that Christ is a collective man, a corporate man. Just as the old man includes Adam and all his descendants, the new man includes Christ and all His believers.

We were made as parts of the first Adam, and now we have been regenerated as parts of the last Adam to be the expression of God in Christ. With the first Adam, everything is a figure and is not real. But with the last Adam, everything is real. If you are merely a person of the first Adam, you do not have anything real. After you have been regenerated to become a part of the last Adam, there is something real within you.

God also created a bride, a wife, to match man, to be the helpmate to man, the counterpart of man, and this counterpart was his increase. A wife is a counterpart and an increase to her husband. A man needs a wife to match him, to be his counterpart. A watermelon cut in two halves is a picture of a wife and a husband. One half is the husband and the other half is the wife, and when you put the two halves together, you have the whole person. As a man, you need a wife to match you to be your counterpart, to make you whole, to make you complete, and to be your increase. The man created by God is a figure of Christ. He needs a counterpart. This simply means that Christ, the new man in this universe, needs a counterpart. The church is the bride of Christ, the counterpart to match Christ.

The Scriptures reveal how much Christ loves the church and desires to have the church. This is why the enemy always does his best to spoil the church. The church is the desire of Christ's heart. Ephesians 5:25 tells us that Christ loved the church and gave Himself up for her. We may only have the thought that Christ loves sinners, so He died for us. We forget that Christ loved the church, so He died on the cross for the church, which is His counterpart.

Therefore, in the types in God's creation, there are the man and the bride, the counterpart, to match the man. This counterpart is something out of man. She is not an addition but an increase. Similarly, the church is not something added to Christ but something increased out of Christ. A man needs a body to express himself and a wife to make him complete. A head without a body is frightening because it is not a real or proper man. Yet today many Christians have the thought that as long as we have Christ as the Head, everything is all right. However, Christ is not only the Head. He also includes the Body, the church. Our Christ must be the Head with the Body.

If we have only a Christian life, that is not good enough. We need the church life. We need to experience Christ as our life, and we also need the experience of the church life. A complete person is a person with a head and a proper body. We need a proper church life to match our Christian life. We need Christ as the Head and the church as the Body.

God created Adam, the husband, but God gave Adam an increase, which was Eve, his wife. Brothers, you cannot live just by yourself as a bachelor. Sooner or later you have to be married. Although some remain unmarried, that is an exception. That is not natural. Spiritually and naturally, you have to marry. This also means that as a Christian, living a proper Christian life, you need the church life. Your spiritual nature within says that you need the church life. A born-again Christian, a spiritual Christian, always longs to have a church life. If you do not have a church life, you have no rest. You are not satisfied. You need both Christ as the Head and the church as the Body.

HOW THE CHURCH COMES INTO BEING
AND IS BUILT UP

Now we have to see how the church comes into being and how the church can be built up as an increase to Christ, a living bride to match Christ, a counterpart of Christ. In order to see this, we need to pay full attention to how Eve, the wife of Adam, came into being. God took a part, a rib, out of Adam, and God built that rib, that piece of bone, into a woman, the increase of Adam to be his wife (Gen. 2:22).

After God created Adam, He saw that Adam as a bachelor, as a single person, was not good enough. Adam needed someone to match him. God had the intention to make a wife for Adam, but He first put Adam to a test. God wanted Adam to realize his need, so He brought all the living creatures to Adam to test him. Adam, by his wisdom, gave every creature a name, but he did not see anything that was good enough to match him. Adam did not find his helpmate among the creatures. None of the created things was qualified to match Adam, because none of them was something out of Adam. They were outside of Adam. God caused Adam to sleep, took a rib out of his side, and built that rib into a wife for Adam. When Adam awoke, he looked at Eve and said, "This is now bone of my bones, and flesh of my flesh" (Gen. 2:23). Thus, Adam found a wife to match him, and the two became one flesh, one body.

In the whole universe, there are thousands of items created by God. It is as if God brought all these things to His Son, Christ, and Christ said, "There is none good enough to match Me. I have to go to the cross and be broken by God." When He was nailed on the cross and broken, blood and water came out of His side (John 19:34). Blood is for redemption, and water is for giving life. On the one hand, He redeems us by His blood, and on the other hand, He generates us, gives life to us.

The bone taken out of Adam signifies the resurrection life of Christ, a life that can stand any kind of opposition or attack. On the cross none of the Lord's bones were broken (John 19:36). His flesh, which typifies the human nature, was broken, but His bone, which typifies the divine life, the resurrection life, could never be broken. It is from this resurrection life, from this bone, that the church comes into being. This resurrection life of Christ becomes the church, just as the bone of Adam became the wife of Adam. The church is something produced out of the resurrection life, the divine life, the eternal life, the uncreated life of Christ.

The church is not of the old creation. The church is of the crucified and resurrected Christ. The church is something out of Christ Himself. The resurrection life has been imparted into us. Within us there is a part of Christ, and that very part is a part of the church of Christ. All the parts of Christ in the real believers added together equal the church. The church is something out of Christ, a part of Christ, the increase of Christ, the counterpart of Christ, the one who can match Christ.

The church must be like Christ because the church is a part of Christ. We have to realize, by this revelation, that the church is nothing less than Christ. Anything that is less than Christ cannot be the church. The church is a part of Christ increased as the Body to match Christ. Anything in the old creation, regardless of how good it is, cannot be added to the church. It is foreign to the church. None of us has the right to bring anything that is outside of Christ into the church. The real church is something of Christ as a part of Christ.

This vision will control us and keep us from trying to bring anything outside of Christ into the church. Whenever you are going to suggest or bring something to the church, you have to ask yourself before the Lord, "Is this something of Christ as a part of Christ?" If it is not, you have to forget about it. This is vital. The church has been corrupted and divided by foreign elements. Many foreign things that were brought into the church have damaged, spoiled, and even disembodied the church.

No foreign, inorganic element can be put into our physical body or it will damage our body, yet this is what many have done to the church. The church is something out of Christ and a part of Christ. None of us has the right to bring something which is not Christ or which is less than Christ into the Body of Christ. If we try to bring something foreign into the Body of Christ, that will damage, kill, and divide the church.

We need to bring Christ as the life supply, the food, to feed the members of the Body for the growth, the building up, of the Body. The church will be increased in life by feeding on Christ. The church is absolutely something out of Christ, as a part of Christ, so the church is the increase of Christ, a counterpart, a bride, a wife, to be married to Christ. We need to pray for the Lord to show us the central thought of God and how the church comes into being. If we are going to allow the Lord to recover His testimony, we have to see all these things in the spirit.

CHAPTER FIVE

BEING TRANSFORMED BY THE SUPPLY OF LIFE TO BECOME PRECIOUS MATERIAL FOR GOD'S BUILDING

Scripture Reading: Gen. 2:8-17; Rev. 22:1-2

CHRIST THE REALITY

We have to see that all the things in the old creation created by God are not the real things but are figures and types of Christ. During the initial years of my Christian life, I did not have such a realization. However, the more I have been following the Lord, the more I have realized, on the one hand by experience and on the other hand by the revelation of the holy Word, that all the things of this universe in the old creation are nothing but figures and types of Christ. Figures and types are not the real things. The photo of a certain person is not the real person. Christ is the reality of all the positive things in creation.

There are two creations: the first creation, which is the old creation, and the second creation, which is the new creation. The old creation is a figure, a type, and the new creation is the reality. Within all the things of the old creation there is nothing of Christ, but with everything in the new creation, Christ is within as the essence, substance, and reality. For instance, we were made in the old creation according to the image of Christ, so we had the form and the image of Christ, but at that time we did not have the nature of Christ. We did not have anything real of Christ. But when we were regenerated, re-created in a new way, we received Christ into us. Now we have not only the form, the appearance, and the image of Christ but also the essence, substance, nature, life, and person of Christ within us. Furthermore, we are looking to the day when the whole universe will be full of Christ in the new heaven and new earth.

MAN BEING AN EMPTY VESSEL TO CONTAIN CHRIST

Man in the old creation was but a form, an empty vessel, to contain Christ. If man would take Christ, then even the animals would have taken Him. If man would reject Christ, then the animals would also reject Him. This is because man is the head of the old creation. Also, we Christians as regenerated persons are the firstfruits of the new creation (James 1:18). We were put into a position to take the lead to receive Christ as our life. The whole old creation is a form, an empty vessel, to contain Christ, with man as the center and as the leader.

Genesis 1 shows that God created the whole universe as an empty vessel in form, in image, in appearance, without anything as the content. We can use a glove as an illustration. A glove is an empty vessel to contain a hand. In every respect a glove has the form of the hand, yet it does not have the hand within as its content. In the first chapter of Genesis you have only the empty glove, the empty form, the empty universe.

In Genesis 2 we are told that man as the leader, the center, and the head of the old creation was made in a way to receive something else. After the creation of man, God told him only how to eat. This simply means that man has to receive something else, something that he does not have, and this very thing will become himself. Dietitians say that we are what we eat. What we eat is what we become. Man was created to receive the Triune God as his spiritual food so that God could become his constitution.

If we draw a picture of the universe, we can show thousands of items as the environment with man in the center, and this man has a mouth to receive the tree of life. After the creation of man as the center, this center with a mouth was put in front of the tree of life, which was edible. The tree of life is a symbol of the Triune God to be our life and life supply. Man is in the center to take the lead to receive the Triune God for the whole universe, just as our mouth takes the lead to receive food for our whole body. After our mouth receives the food, our whole body also receives it. God created the heavens and the earth, with the vegetable life, the animal life, and thousands of things as an environment. In the very center God prepared a garden. In the center of the garden there was the tree of life, and man was put there as the center of the old creation with a mouth to receive something he did not have. Moreover, this very thing which he was to receive would become himself. Thus, man is an empty vessel, an empty container, with an opening to receive the Triune God, who is symbolized by the tree of life. After man receives the Triune God, the Triune God will be digested by him to become his very essence.

Opposite the tree of life, there was another tree—the tree of the knowledge of good and evil—as a test to man. We have to be careful about what we are going to receive. If we receive the tree of life, we will have God as our life and life supply. If we receive the other tree, the tree of knowledge, we will have Satan, the enemy of God, and death. There are two possibilities for one mouth. There is the possibility to receive God or to receive Satan.

TREASURING THE FLOW OF LIFE

If you receive God, you will have the life of God. Then you will have a flow, a stream, a river, of living water within you. In Genesis 2:10-14 we see that by the side of the tree of life there is one river flowing with four heads toward the four directions of the whole earth. When you receive Christ as your life, there is something within you flowing all the time as a stream of living water.

Christians are living persons. They are very active and very positive because there is another life within them that is living, moving, acting, and energizing. There is only one way for you to check whether you are proper as a Christian. That way is to check if you have the living stream flowing within you all the time. Do you have the living flow, the living stream, within you at this very moment? By our experience we know that there is a flow, a current, of the life of God.

When we are regenerated, we have something within us that is living, acting, moving, and energizing as an inner flow.

One day a servant of the Lord whom I knew well told me that in a certain place at a certain time he desperately felt that the stream within him stopped. A year later I met him again, and he told me, "Brother, even up to this day, the stream, the flow, within me has not been recovered." Then he said, "Brother Lee, this morning I got up early, about five o'clock, to cry to the Lord, 'Lord, why has the flow within stopped? For more than a year, even up to this day, it has not been recovered. O Lord, why?'"

As a Christian, a reborn one, you should have the divine life within you flowing all the time. If the flow is stopped, that means you are wrong. As a husband or a wife, you may quarrel about who is right and who is wrong. While you are quarreling, however, the current within you is stopped. You are right, but the current is stopped. You are right and everything is to your credit, but there is a debit within you. As far as the current is concerned, there is a debit. The heavenly bank would not credit you. The more you quarrel, the more you reason with others, the more your inner conscience tells you that the current within you is stopped.

Sometimes you have another kind of experience. While you are trying to quarrel, there is a frustration within you. That frustration is the inhibiting of the flow of the life stream. If you would go along with this inner sense and say, "Lord, I will stop everything," you will sense how living the flow is within you. You may give up your reasoning, but you have the living flow, the current, the fellowship, the communion, the stream, of the life of God. What good is it to be right yet not have the flow? As long as you have the divine life, you should have the divine flow. If you are in the communion, the fellowship, with God, you have the flow. Otherwise, you are out of the fellowship.

THE ISSUE OF THE FLOW OF LIFE

The picture in Genesis 2 further shows us that out of the flow, three precious items come into being. These three items are gold, bdellium (pearl), and onyx stone. There are one tree and one river, but three items. The number *three* points to the Divine Trinity. If you have God as the tree of life, you will have the divine stream flowing within you all the time. Then the issue, the result, will be three items of precious things. Man was a piece of clay, formed out of the dust of the ground, but before him was the tree of life with a flow of living water issuing in three precious items. This picture shows that we can be transformed into precious materials for God's building by partaking of the tree of life and enjoying the inner flow of the river of water of life.

At the beginning of the Scriptures, there was a man by the name of Adam. That man was of dust, a man of clay, an earthen man. But at the end of the whole Scriptures, that is, at the end of the book of Revelation, there is another man, a corporate man, a collective man, with the names of the twelve tribes and of the twelve apostles. With this collective man, this corporate man, everything is gold, pearl, and precious stones. That corporate man is the holy city, the New Jerusalem. The city itself is gold, the entrances of the city are pearls, and the wall with its foundations is precious stones.

The man in the first creation is a man of dust, but the man in the second creation is a man of gold, of pearls, and of precious stones. In the first two chapters of the Scriptures, that man was the old man in the old creation. In the last two chapters, this man is the new man in the new creation. Man as a piece of clay is transformed, transfigured, into precious materials by taking the Triune God as life.

By taking the tree of life and by having the flow of the divine river, we are first regenerated. Regeneration is a change, a transformation, a transfiguration, in our spirit. After regeneration, gradually we have to be transformed, and finally our vile body will be changed, transfigured, into a glorious body. We have three parts: spirit, soul, and body. In our spirit we have been regenerated. From that time onward we have to be transformed in the soul—in the mind, emotion, and will. Then eventually, when the Lord comes back, our body will be transfigured. First, we are regenerated in the spirit; second, we are being transformed in the soul; and lastly, we will be transfigured in our body. We were made persons of clay, but by taking God as life and by having the divine river flowing within us, we can be regenerated and transformed into gold, pearl, and precious stones.

All these precious materials are something of the Triune God. The first item is of the Father, the second item is of the Son, and the third item is of the Spirit. God the Father to us is the divine nature as the gold. After we have been regenerated, we have the life of God and the divine nature of God, which is signified by gold. In the types of the Scriptures, gold signifies the divine nature, whereas wood signifies the human nature. For instance, in the Old Testament there is acacia wood overlaid with gold to make many items within the tabernacle. Acacia wood signifies the human nature of Christ, and gold signifies the divine nature. Gold is God the Father's divine nature. Gold is not an element that has been transformed.

However, pearl is different. Pearl is not something created by God. It comes out of a pearl-bearing oyster. The oyster is hurt, wounded, by a grain of sand. Then the secretion of the oyster gradually transforms the grain of sand into a pearl. The oyster signifies Christ. Christ lived in the death waters, in this world of death. He was wounded by us, a piece of sand, and He secretes His life over us to make us precious pearls for the building of God's eternal expression. By Christ's wound and life we as little grains of sand are regenerated to be pearls. Hence, this is the work of the Second of the Godhead. The pearl signifies God the Son as regeneration to us. Our regeneration transpired in the Son, by the Son, and with the Son.

Now we need to consider the significance of the precious stones. Precious stones are not created by God. They have been transformed, transfigured, from some other material. A piece of coal becomes a diamond, a precious stone, through a tremendous amount of heat and pressure over a long period of time. Since we have been born again, the Holy Spirit has been trying His best to put us under a certain kind of pressure and into a certain kind of burning for our transformation. Do you consider yourself to be precious, good, and nice? Truthfully, I do not feel that I am so nice. Many times I look at myself as a piece of black, dark coal. I have been regenerated, and I have the nature of God. There is no doubt about this, but I am still a piece of coal or a piece of clay. I need pressure and burning. The Holy Spirit always tries His best, if we are available, to put us under a certain pressure and burning for our transformation. Then we become the precious material for His building.

CHAPTER SIX

THE PROCESS FOR THE SUBDUING
OF THE SERPENT

Scripture Reading: Gen. 3:1, 13-15; John 3:14; 12:31-32; Rev. 20:1-3

As we have seen, the first two chapters of the Scriptures give us the blueprint of God's plan, and the last two chapters of the Scriptures show us a picture of the consummation of God's plan. If you cut off the first two chapters with the blueprint and the last two chapters with the picture and read from the third chapter of Genesis to the twentieth chapter of Revelation, you will realize that the greater part of the Scripture starts with the serpent (Gen. 3:1) and ends with the ancient serpent (Rev. 20:2). This shows us that after the blueprint of the divine plan had been revealed, the serpent came in right away to damage, to poison, the vessel created by God for Himself.

SATAN INJECTING HIMSELF INTO MAN

God's central thought is to put Himself into all His creation as the vessel with man as the center and all the other things as an environment, an attachment, to this vessel. But before God put Himself into this vessel, Satan, the enemy of God, came in as the serpent to damage, to poison, the vessel. He knew that man is the center of the vessel of the old creation, so he came in to inject his poison into the center of this vessel. If you look at the Scriptures with this point of view, you will understand why the serpent came in such a way. In order to inject something into a physical body, you always choose a soft place. A soft place is so easy to inject something into. The enemy, the serpent, is very subtle. He knows quite well which part of the old creation is the softest; it is the females. The sisters are too soft. Because they are so soft, they are good for the enemy to come in and inject something. Many times I told people that if you are going to contact the sisters, do not reason with them or argue with them. Just drop two tears; you will convince them because they are so soft. The enemy did the same in principle. He came in to inject himself through the soft part, the weak part, of humanity, and he succeeded.

From that time on Satan has been mixed with humanity. In the human nature there is something of the serpent. In the human nature there is something satanic, something that is Satan himself. When the Lord was on this earth, He scolded people by calling them "offspring of vipers" (Matt. 3:7; 12:34) and "brood of vipers" (23:33), that is, children of the serpent. Furthermore, He told the Jews that they were of their father the devil (John 8:44). In other words, they were the children of the devil because the life, the nature, the substance, of the serpent has been injected into the human nature. We must realize what the fall of man means. It does not only mean that man did something wrong against the law of God; that is too objective. The fall of man is also very subjective in that something of Satan has been mixed with man.

Do you know what the difference is between the body and the flesh? The body was made by God as a pure vessel to contain the soul, while the flesh is the body mixed with the nature of Satan, becoming something very sinful. If you read Romans 7, you will realize that sin dwells in the members of the body (vv. 17, 20, 23). In Romans 6, 7, and 8 *sin,* singular in number, denotes the life and nature of Satan. In fact, in these three chapters, sin is a person, the embodiment of Satan, and is living and acting. It can reign as king (6:12); it can rule over you, control you, and lord it over you (v. 14); and it can become your master and make you a slave (v. 20). Sin, which is the life and nature of the devil, is in the body. Therefore the body was changed in nature because something of Satan was injected into it, causing it to be mixed with Satan. If you read the Scriptures carefully, you will see that from Genesis 3 all the things on the negative side came from the injection of the serpent, from Satan.

CHRIST COMING AS THE SEED OF THE WOMAN
AND THE BRASS SERPENT

At the very juncture when man fell, God came in and promised that One would come as the seed of woman (Gen. 3:15). Therefore, we are clearly told in the Scriptures that the Son of God, Jesus Christ, was born through a virgin (Isa. 7:14; Matt. 1:23; Gal. 4:4); His birth was not of a human father. He is the real seed of woman who dealt with the serpent by bruising his head, that is, by putting him to death. In order to kill a serpent, you do not deal with its tail, its body. Rather, you have to deal with its head. If you hit its head with a stone, you will put it to death. It is the seed of the woman who bruised the head of the serpent, who put Satan to death. Due to Satan's subtlety today, many people, even in Christianity, do not recognize that the Lord Jesus was born of a virgin. The enemy knows that the seed of woman refers to Christ. One day the Lord came as the seed of the woman to bruise the head of the serpent, that is, to put Satan to death.

In John 3:14 the Lord told us that as Moses lifted up the serpent in the wilderness, so must the Son of Man be lifted up. The story of the type of the brass serpent is recorded in Numbers 21:4-9. Moses lifted up the brass serpent in the wilderness in order to deliver the people of Israel from the poison of the serpents. At that very time, the people of Israel in the eyes of God were just like serpents because they had been poisoned by the serpents. When God provided a deliverance, that is, a deliverer, that deliverer was lifted up in the form of a serpent to be their substitute. Because they were serpents in the eyes of God, their substitute needed to be in the form of a serpent. The Lord was lifted up on the cross with the human nature in the form of a serpent. I would ask you, "Was the One who was nailed on the cross on Calvary a man or a serpent?" He was a man with the form of a serpent. Jesus was a man crucified on the cross, yet He was crucified there in the form of a serpent. The One who was lifted up was only in the form of the serpent, without the nature, the life,

and the poison of the serpent. Romans 8:3 tells us that the
Lord Jesus came in the likeness of the flesh of sin. He had
only the form of the flesh of sin but not its nature. So when
the Lord was lifted up on the cross, not only man but also
Satan was dealt with. When fallen man, fallen humanity, was
dealt with on the cross by the death of the Lord, Satan was
also dealt with.

Thirty years ago I listened to a message given by Brother
Watchman Nee. He told us that Satan thought that it was for-
tuitous for him to gain man, to possess man, and to put
himself into man as a resident within him. Brother Nee said
that, on the contrary, this was a pity to Satan because having
come into man, he became located. It is hard to catch a mouse
at large, but if you can locate it, it is easy to catch. When Satan
entered into the human nature, he was located and bound
with the human nature. On the day that the Lord took the
human nature to the cross, He simply put Satan, who was
within the human nature, on the cross. It was easy for the
Lord to deal with Satan simply by His death on the cross.
When the Lord was lifted up, man, humanity with the satanic
nature, was dealt with there, and Satan was also dealt with by
the death of the Lord on the cross. Therefore we are told that
Christ destroyed, annulled, the enemy of God by His death on
the cross (Heb. 2:14). In this way Satan has been cast out.

FIVE CENTRAL MATTERS IN THE SCRIPTURES

From the time of the cross, all that the Lord has done and
is still doing on the negative side is to execute the judgment
that He accomplished on the cross, that is, to execute the
judgment on Satan. Satan has been cast out; that is something accomplished judicially, but once a case is tried in court
and judgment is declared, there is the need of the execution.
The execution of a judgment always requires executioners.
After the judgment on the cross, the Lord did and is still
doing many things on the negative side to execute the judgment until the time when He will have the adequate
cooperation of the Christian "executioners." When He has
adequate Christian executioners to cooperate with Him, then

He will come to bind the serpent and cast him into the bottomless pit (Rev. 20:2-3). That will be the end of the serpent.

This is the whole story of the greater part of the Scriptures from Genesis 3 through Revelation 20. However, this is only on the negative side, from the enemy's sneaking in to the enemy's being cast out. In this long period four things also happened on the positive side. On the negative side the Lord came to deal with Satan, but on the positive side the Lord first came to give Himself to us through death and resurrection and in the Spirit and in the Word. In order to eat a chicken, you cannot simply bring it to your dining table. First you have to kill it, and then you have to cook it. After cooking the chicken, you can then receive it in another form; this is a picture of resurrection. You can now put the cooked chicken on a plate on the dining table because it is ready to be eaten. When the Lord Jesus was killed, He was "cooked." Have you realized that the Lord was "cooked" in the "fire?" He was prepared, and now He is ready for us in the Spirit and in the Word. The Spirit is the "plate," and the Word is the "dining table." When you come to the Word, you come to the dining table, and when you contact the Spirit, you contact the plate, and the food is on the plate. The Lord went through death and was resurrected; that is, He was slain and cooked. He has been put in the Spirit and has been embodied in the Word. He was prepared and has been presented to us. Therefore, the Gospels tell us that "all things are ready" (Matt. 22:2-14). This is the first matter on the positive side.

The second positive matter is that you need to come and feast. This is to repent and believe in the Lord Jesus, receiving Him. This is to be saved. The first matter is that the feast has been prepared and all things are ready, while the second matter is that you have to come to take Him, to receive Him.

The third matter is that, after being regenerated and saved, after coming to the Lord, you have to feed, even to feast, on Him day by day that you may grow and be transformed. In today's Christianity, after people are saved, they are taught many things. They are taught to do this and to do that. I must tell you that this is wrong. After you have been saved and regenerated, after you have come to the Lord, the only thing you have to do is to feed on the Lord day by day that you may grow by the Lord and in the Lord and that you may be transformed in Christ. The last item is that you have to be built up together as one Body. This means that you need to have a church life and to be a living member functioning in the Body.

In summary, on the negative side there is only one item: to deal with Satan, to cast out the serpent. On the positive side we have four matters. First, the Lord Jesus died and resurrected; He was transfigured; He has been prepared, and He is ready for us. Second, we have to come to Him, to believe in Him, to receive Him. Third, we have to feed on Him, fellowship with Him, and commune with Him all the time. In this way we can grow and be transformed into His image. Fourth, we have to be built up together as the Body to have a church life and be the living members functioning in the Body. If people ask what the Scripture teaches and tells us, we have to tell them that its first two chapters are the blueprint of the divine plan, its last two chapters give us a picture of what God has been doing, and the greater part in between shows us five things, one on the negative side and four on the positive side. On the negative side, Christ came to deal with Satan, to cast out the serpent. On the positive side, Christ has been prepared for us, we must come to receive Him, enjoy Him, experience Him, and feed on Him to grow and be transformed, and we must be built up together as the church, the Body. This is what the entire Scripture says. Now you can see the central thought of God, what God is seeking. Eventually, we see that God is seeking after a building. Therefore, the picture in the last two chapters shows us that the ultimate consummation of God's work throughout the generations simply will be a building. Do you have a clear vision of this? What is your goal as a Christian? What is your direction as a believer in Christ? You must have this vision with such a building as the goal, the aim, and the direction.

CHRIST ON THE CROSS
DEALING WITH SIX ITEMS RELATED TO SATAN

After Satan came in, he brought in many items. First, Satan brought sin and death to us (Rom. 5:12). Following this, he constituted sinful man. The man created by God was pure, but after the fall, man was injected with Satan, so man became sinful and was constituted a sinner (5:19a). Furthermore, he brought in the world, the human life in human society. Do you realize that human society is a world under Satan? The world is a satanic system. The Greek word for *world, kosmos,* simply means a system. The enemy, Satan, systematized the human race with the human society. When you come into human society, there are many systems systematizing you. Education is a system; marriage is also a system. However, this does not mean that education and marriage are wrong. Rather, marriage has been utilized by the enemy as a system to systematize people. You need to get married, but do not be systematized. You may ask what the difference is between marriage and the system of marriage. If you consider the marriage of Isaac and Rebecca, you will be able to see the difference. Isaac married Rebecca; that was all. It was so simple. Today, however, there is a system of marriage. When people are married, they come not only into marriage but also into the system of marriage. Isaac came into marriage, but he was not systematized by marriage. I do not say that you should not marry. On the contrary, I have said that you need to be increased. However, you should not be systematized by anything of the human life.

All things of the proper human life are of God, but all these proper things have been utilized by the enemy as systems to systematize people. Hence, the human life systematized by the enemy simply becomes a world, a system. People have no liberty, no freedom, to serve God because they are so systematized. This does not mean that the young people should not go to school. Rather, I encourage you to go to school. However, do not be systematized by your degree, even by your Ph.D. Likewise, you must use money, but do not be systematized by it. You also need to clothe yourself. This is something ordained by God, but the enemy has utilized the matter of clothing to systematize people. Many worldly people do not have the freedom, the liberty, to serve the Lord simply because they have been systematized by their clothing. Some people spend hours in dressing themselves, but they would not spend one minute to read the Word. They spend many hours to go shopping for their clothing, but they do not come to the meetings. They serve clothing, but they do not serve God. To dress ourselves is not something of the world, but to be systematized by dressing is absolutely something of the world. That is something worldly.

Therefore, we see that with Satan sin came in, death came in, sinners were constituted, and a world was formed, organized, and systematized. In addition, there is the kingdom of darkness, that is, the kingdom of Satan with the rulers, the authorities, the world-rulers of this darkness, the spiritual forces of evil in the heavenlies (Eph. 6:12). All these things are related to Satan. This is a satanic group consisting of six items: Satan, sin, death, sinners, the systematized world, and the kingdom of darkness. On the negative side, these are the matters that the Scriptures are concerned with. By the cross the Lord put the enemy, Satan, to death (Heb. 2:14). He also died as the One who was made sin for us (2 Cor. 5:21), and He died for our sins (1 Cor. 15:3). All sins are the fruits of sin. Thus, on the cross He solved the problem of sin with its sins. Not only so, the Lord tasted death on the cross (Heb. 2:9) and thus solved the problem of death. Furthermore, on the cross the Lord has crucified the sinful man. Galatians 2:20a says that we have been crucified with Him, and Romans 6:6 says that our old man has been crucified with Christ. Then, what about the world? The world has also been judged by the Lord on the cross (John 12:31; Gal. 6:14b). When man was put to death on the cross, Satan, who was within man, was also put to death, and the world which belongs to Satan was judged on the cross. Moreover, according to Colossians 2:15, the kingdom of darkness with the rulers and authorities was stripped off by Christ on the cross. Thus, it is only by the cross that the Lord has dealt with and is still dealing with this satanic group of items.

By this summary you should be clear what the central thought of God is. The central thought of God is not merely to put away sins, to forgive sins, or to save and deliver us. The central thought of God is that Christ has to be wrought into us, and we have to be built up together with others as the

Body, which is the corporate expression of God in Christ, to be a spiritual building, the New Jerusalem. This is the central thought, and it is the direction, the goal, the aim, toward which God is working.

CHAPTER SEVEN

GOD'S ULTIMATE INTENTION— CHRIST AND THE CHURCH

Scripture Reading: Gen. 28:12, 16-19, 22; Exo. 40:34; 1 Kings 8:10-11; Matt. 16:16-18; 1 Tim. 3:15-16; Eph. 5:32

Ephesians 5:32 speaks of a great mystery. Christ with the church is the great mystery in this universe. In these messages our burden is the central thought of God. We have seen clearly from the revelation of the Scriptures that the central thought of God is Christ as the expression of God with His Body, which is the church. So the central thought of God is Christ and the church, or we may say Christ with the church. This is the center of the divine mind, the divine thought, which is clearly seen in the blueprint of the divine plan unveiled in the first two chapters of the Bible. In the picture in Revelation 21 and 22, the last two chapters of the Scriptures, we can also see that the eternal purpose, the ultimate intention, of God is to have Christ expressed through the Body. Hence, Christ and His Body, which is the church, are the great mystery as the central thought of God.

I was a young man when I was saved. Immediately after I was saved, I loved the Word of the Lord very much. Day by day I studied it with great diligence. Later I acquired a great number of books about the Scriptures. All those books told me the same thing, that is, that Christ is the subject and the center of all the Scriptures. At that time I was very happy to know this, and I stressed this very much. Christ is the subject, the center, and the contents of all the Scriptures! Later, however, I found out that this was short of something. In the Scriptures we are told clearly that Christ is the Head (Eph. 1:22; Col. 1:18). Just as a head needs a body, Christ as the

Head needs the Body. We are also told that Christ is the Husband (Eph. 5:24-25), and a husband needs a wife. Christ is the divine Husband, the real man. None of us, including the brothers, is a man. We are all really females. Christ is the real man to gain a bride (John 3:29). As the real man, He needs a bride. Therefore, the Scriptures do not reveal to us the Head without the Body. It reveals to us the Head with the Body, Christ with the church. Moreover, it reveals to us a couple, not just the Husband alone, but the Husband with the wife.

If you would read your Bible carefully once more, you will realize that the center, the subject, and the contents of all the Scriptures is Christ with the church, the Head with the Body, the Husband with the wife. How can I come to speak with my head and leave my body in my apartment? You can never separate a body from the head nor the head from a body. One thing I appreciate about this country is that wives always go together with their husbands. It is not so in China. In China, the wives are separated from the husbands. If the husbands sit in the front, all the wives sit at the rear. That is not scriptural. If you read the Scriptures, you will see that where Christ is, there is the church; where the Head is, there is the Body; and where the Husband is, there is the bride.

Brothers and sisters, the central thought of God is that Christ must have a church as His Body, His Bride, His increase, and His counterpart to express God in a corporate way. In all the Scriptures, nothing is more important or vital than this. Nothing is more central than this. This is the very central thought of God. If you ask me what the Lord is seeking after today, I must tell you that the Lord is seeking nothing other than the church as the Body, the bride, and the increase to match Christ and to express Christ in a corporate way. This is the ultimate intention of God.

THE FULL MEASURE OF THE REVELATION OF CHRIST

Let us now see something of Christ and the church in a very brief way from the sixty-six books of the Bible from Genesis to Revelation. We all know that Christ is the center, but we must realize that Christ is the center with the church. On the fourth day of creation, there is the sun with the moon and all the stars. The sun is a type of Christ; Christ is the Sun of righteousness (Mal. 4:2). The church as the moon reflects His light, and all the saints are the stars. Therefore, in the first chapter of the Bible there is Christ with the church, including all the saints.

Then, in the second chapter, there is Adam with Eve, the man with the wife. As we have seen, Adam is a figure, and he has an increase, a bride, a counterpart, a part of himself. Here also is Christ and the church. Then, in the third chapter, there is the seed of the woman, that is, Christ born of a virgin. As you read on, you will see a number of types of Christ, but we will now skip to the time of Jacob. If you read Genesis carefully, you will notice that the revelation concerning Christ does not come to a full measure until Jacob, because Jacob brought in a house for God (Gen. 28:10-22). In the Bible, the Lord does not speak of the house of Abraham or the house of Isaac. However, the Scriptures often refer to the house of Jacob, or the house of Israel. Abraham seemingly was an individual person, and Isaac apparently was the same. But with Jacob it is not a matter of an individual person but a matter of a house—the house of Jacob, the house of Israel. Therefore, the revelation of Christ came to a full measure with Jacob.

What is the revelation which Jacob received at that time concerning Christ? In his dream, Jacob saw a ladder (Gen. 28:12). In John 1:51 the Lord said to Nathanael, "Truly, truly, I say to you, You shall see heaven opened and the angels of God ascending and descending on the Son of Man." In this way the Lord Jesus referred to this ladder, telling us that this ladder is Himself. He is the heavenly ladder that brings heaven to earth. Jacob received a revelation in a dream concerning Christ as the heavenly ladder bringing heaven to earth. At that time, as a young man, Jacob did something very wonderful. He took the stone which he had used as a pillow, set it up for a pillar, and poured oil upon it (Gen. 28:11, 18). Then he called the name of that place Bethel (v. 19), that is, the house of God. He not only said that that place was the house of God, but he even said that the pillar, the stone on which the oil was poured, was the house of God (v. 22). Do you realize that in this picture there is Christ and there is also the church? The heavenly ladder is Christ, and the house of God made with the stone upon which oil was poured is the church.

We have to believe that what that naughty young Jacob did was something done through him by the Holy Spirit. Jacob was homeless, and he was a wanderer, yet he forgot about being homeless. Rather, he cared very much about the house of God. Instead of saying, "This pillar will be my house," he said, "This is...the house of God" (v. 17). Similarly, in Matthew 16 when Peter received the revelation concerning Christ, he said, "You are the Christ, the Son of the living God" (v. 16), the heavenly ladder that brings heaven to earth. The Lord right away told Peter, "And I also say to you that you are Peter [or, a stone], and upon this rock I will build My church" (v. 18). If you compare these two visions, you will realize that in principle they are exactly the same. When you truly know Christ as the heavenly One, a vision will come to you in which a pillar is set up, oil is poured upon it, and Bethel comes forth.

The pillar of stone signifies a regenerated and transformed person. Originally and naturally, we were not pillars of stone but pieces of clay—at most, pillars of salt, as Lot's wife became a pillar of salt (Gen. 19:26). But praise the Lord, we have been regenerated and we are being transformed. Now we are stones, and the Holy Spirit as the oil is poured upon us. Out of this, the house of God comes into being. All these things happen when you see Christ as the heavenly One and realize Christ as the One who brings God to man and brings heaven to earth. Christ is the One who opens the heavens and brings heaven to earth and God to man. When you realize Christ as such a One, you will sense that there is a great change, a regeneration, even a transformation within you. You will be a stone for the building of the church. The more you realize Christ as the heavenly One who brings heaven to earth and who brings God to man, the more you will be transformed from a piece of clay into a stone, and the more you will be built up upon the rock.

If you know Christ, you must also realize the church. If you truly know the Head, then, to be sure, you will realize the Body. You may say, "Oh, I am a pitiful sinner, and He is the Savior. He died on the cross for my sins to save me from hell and will bring me to heaven to the heavenly mansion." However, if you only realize Christ as the Savior in such a way, I am afraid that you will never realize something of the church, but if you realize that Christ is the heavenly One who comes to the earth to bring heaven to earth and to bring God to man to be mingled together with man, then there will be a great change within you. There will be a regeneration and a transformation within you. You will be greatly transformed, and you will realize that you are just a stone for the building up of the church upon the rock, which is Christ and the revelation concerning Christ.

ENJOYING AND EXPERIENCING CHRIST
TO BECOME THE CHURCH

Now let us go on from Jacob to Israel, the house of Jacob. The house of Jacob first enjoyed Christ as the Passover lamb (Exo. 12; 1 Cor. 5:7). On the day of the Passover, the Israelites put the blood of the lamb on the two side posts and on the lintels (Exo. 12:7), and they ate the flesh of the lamb (v. 8). This signifies that, on the one hand, they enjoyed the redemption of Christ, while on the other hand, they enjoyed Christ as life and the life supply to them. Furthermore, they enjoyed Christ as the unleavened bread (vv. 15-20). Do you realize what God asked them to do after they enjoyed Christ in such a way? God asked them to set up a tabernacle, to build up a house for Him (25:8). The children of Israel enjoyed and experienced Christ in the way of redemption and in the way of life. Immediately after this, God not only commanded but demanded that they set up a tabernacle as His dwelling place among them. Therefore, here again we have Christ and the church.

If you read the book of Exodus once more, you will realize that all the timber, the boards, and the other materials for the tabernacle are types of aspects of Christ enjoyed by the believers to make them materials for the building of the church. What is the tabernacle? The tabernacle is the enlargement, the increase, of Christ as the lamb. If you enjoy the lamb, I enjoy the lamb, and we all enjoy the lamb, eventually this lamb will become the tabernacle through us. The children of Israel could be enlarged into a tabernacle simply because, in type, they experienced and enjoyed Christ and were united with Christ. They received something of Christ, and this very portion of Christ made them materials for the tabernacle. Today we have Christ and we are the church, not by natural goodness or other natural matters, but by the Christ who is experienced by us. We are the church by Christ being experienced by us and making us the material of the church. Just as the lamb became the tabernacle, Christ enjoyed and experienced by us becomes the church.

If you experience and enjoy Christ, there is truly a longing within you for the church life. If you have a good contact with the Lord Jesus in the morning, I am sure you will come to the church meeting in the evening. You have enjoyed Christ, yet you realize that you must be in the church for your living. This is why, in many cases, we should not talk to people about the church. We should simply help them to realize Christ. The more they realize Christ, the more they will long for the church. The lamb will become the tabernacle, Christ will become the church, but He must be experienced and enjoyed by you. First you have the Passover lamb, and then you will have the tabernacle in the wilderness built up as a dwelling place for God. After the tabernacle was raised up, a number of offerings, typifying Christ, were offered to God. We can never separate Christ, typified by the offerings, from the church, typified by the tabernacle. Where the tabernacle is, there are the offerings. Where the church is, there is Christ, and where Christ is, there is the church.

The entire history of the children of Israel in the Old Testament is a history of the tabernacle and of the temple. In principle, these two are the same. At first the tabernacle was the center of the history of Israel, and later on the temple became the center. This shows us that God's intention is that we experience Christ so that a building may come into existence. This is the central thought of God. The temple came into being through the experience of Christ in type. After the children of Israel were brought into the land of Canaan, after they enjoyed Canaan, and after they experienced all the goodness of Canaan, the temple came forth. Again, Canaan is a type of Christ, and the temple is a type of the church. Just as the temple is the ultimate issue of the experience and enjoyment of the good land, the church is the ultimate issue of the experience and the enjoyment of Christ by the saints. When we enjoy Christ, the church comes out. After the Israelites enjoyed and experienced all the riches, the goodness, of the good land, they built up the temple as the dwelling place for God. This is a picture of the church coming out of Christ, who has been experienced by us.

THE PROBLEM TODAY CONCERNING THE CHURCH

Now we come to the New Testament. The record of the New Testament is a record of the Head with the Body, a record of Christ and the church. Christ is the Head and the church is the Body. A number of years ago, some young people in the Far East claimed that they saw the revelation concerning Christ and the fullness of Christ. They said there was no need to talk about the church because as long as we have Christ, everything is all right. It is absurd to say this. If you truly have the revelation of Christ, you will also have the revelation of the church. You cannot have a revelation concerning the Head without the Body. If you do see something of Christ, the church will follow. In Matthew 16:16 Peter saw the revelation from the heavenly Father concerning Christ. He said, "You are the Christ, the Son of the living God." Then immediately after that, the Lord said, "Upon this rock I will build My church" (v. 18). If you know Christ, surely you will know the church. It is not possible to have the Head without the Body. Look at the writings, the teachings, the preachings, of the apostles, especially the apostle Paul. How much he spoke concerning the Body of Christ! Nearly all the Epistles written by the apostles stress not only Christ the Head but also the church, the Body.

Today the problem among the believers is not mainly concerning Christ but concerning the church. I do not believe that the genuine believers are very wrong concerning Christ, the Head, but unfortunately, most of the believers are wrong with the Body. I have been a Christian for nearly forty years, and I have been serving the Lord for more than thirty years. I have to tell you, I have suffered only a little for the Lord

Himself, but I have suffered very much for the church. Therefore, there is a great problem related to the Body. As long as you simply speak about Christ without mentioning the Body, you will be considered wonderful, but you will be wonderful "in the air," not practically. However, if you are going to speak practically concerning the church, you have to be ready to suffer persecution. Today the subtle enemy, the old serpent, is still trying his best to frustrate, to damage, to spoil, even to kill the church life, the Body of Christ. Do you realize what the Lord said to us? He said, "Upon this rock I will build My church, and the gates of Hades shall not prevail against it" (Matt. 16:18). This proves and reveals to us that the church will be attacked by the gates of Hades, but praise the Lord, we can be at peace. Do not be scared away. You have to take the Lord's word, because He told us clearly that the church built with living stones on this divine rock can never be defeated by the gates of Hades. All the power of death, all the power of hell, and all the power of the satanic forces cannot prevail against the church which is built on the solid rock. Nevertheless, we have to realize that here is a real battle. As long as we are going along with the Body of Christ, we have to be ready to suffer for the Body.

Now you can see that the ultimate intention of God is to have the church built up for Himself and for His Son, as a building for Himself and as a Body, a bride, an increase, for His Son. This is the central thought of God. This is the very central thing which the Lord Himself is seeking after. If we see this, we are ready for the last two chapters of the Scriptures concerning the New Jerusalem. The New Jerusalem is nothing other than the ultimate consummation of the divine work throughout the generations. After the old creation, God's work throughout all the generations is a work for the new creation with a new man—the New Jerusalem—in a new heaven and new earth.

CHAPTER EIGHT

GIFTS, DOCTRINES, LAW, AND RELIGION VERSUS CHRIST

Scripture Reading: 1 Cor. 1:22-24, 30; 2:2; Gal. 1:15-16; 4:19; Col. 1:27; 2:3; 3:11; Heb. 1:2; Eph. 4:13-16

THE CHURCH BEING OF CHRIST, EVEN CHRIST HIMSELF

In this chapter we must see something more important than what we have seen in the previous chapters. We want to see how the church comes into being, how the church grows up, and how the church is built up. As we have said many times, the church is absolutely something of Christ, and strictly speaking, the church is something as Christ. It is not only something of Christ but something as Christ. The church is part of Christ. We have seen that the church is the increase of Christ, something that comes out of Christ to be increased as a bride to match Him. Now we need to go on to see something from the books written by the apostle Paul. Because in Paul's days many things other than Christ had come into the church, the church was greatly damaged, spoiled, and dismembered. The church was even killed by many foreign things. Today the situation is the same.

If we want to speak about the church, we have to know what the real experience of Christ is. First of all, we have to discern the difference between the gifts and Christ. The gifts are things for Christ, but they are not Christ Himself. You may have a certain gift, yet you may have nothing to do with Christ. Do not think that the gifts are Christ. Gifts are things from God, but they are not Christ Himself. We all need to realize this. For instance, the Old Testament speaks of an ass that could speak a human language (Num. 22:28-30). No doubt, that was a miraculous and extraordinary gift. If today an ass spoke in English, the whole city would be excited, and the newspapers would greatly publicize it. However, it would not be something which is Christ Himself. Similarly, although the prophets in the Old Testament time spoke many things concerning Christ, what they had was merely a gift for them to speak for Christ. What they had was not Christ Himself.

Today many Christians pay too much attention to divine healing. I do not like to criticize others, but as one of the Lord's servants I have to be faithful. In these days different ones have asked me what kind of ministry I have. Because I did not know what they meant, I have been bothered by their question. Eventually, I said, "My ministry is a ministry of Christ." Some of them went on to ask, "What do you mean by the ministry of Christ? Do you have a healing ministry?" Sometimes we have healings, but we do not say that our ministry is a healing ministry. Divine healing is not bad or unnecessary. In fact, I myself have experienced divine healing in the past years. Moreover, I have to testify to the Lord's mercy that I have brought divine healing to others, and I have seen a good number of believers among us receiving divine healing. However, dear brothers and sisters, you have to realize that divine healing is something other than Christ. You may have divine healing, yet you may not have Christ.

In the past years I saw a number of people who received divine healing yet did not know Christ. Healing is one matter, while the Healer is another. Do you want the Healer or the healing? Likewise, gifts are one matter, but the Giver is another. Do you want the gifts or the Giver? I am sorry to say, however, that today many brothers and sisters pay too much attention to the gifts but pay very little attention to the Giver. The gifts are for the Giver, but today the gifts have become a frustration to the Giver. The gifts should be a help that brings people to the Giver, but today people are content with the gifts, and they forget about the Giver. In the Old Testament we have the story of Rebekah in Genesis 24. When the old servant of Abraham found Rebekah and presented to her a considerable number of gifts from Isaac (v. 53), she was not satisfied with the gifts. Those gifts served only as a reminder to remind Rebekah of Isaac, the giver of the gifts. Hence, Rebekah agreed right away to go with the old servant to be with Isaac (v. 58). Today, however, many people are satisfied with the gifts, and they have no heart and even no desire to seek the Giver. We know the story of Rebekah is a type. The old servant is a type of the Holy Spirit sent down by the heavenly Father to seek us as the heavenly Rebekah to marry Christ as the heavenly Isaac. When the Holy Spirit comes to us, He often comes with some gifts, but all these gifts are reminders of Christ, the Giver. When you receive a gift, you should not be satisfied with the gift. You must remember to seek the Giver, who is Christ Himself. By this you can see the difference between the gifts and the Giver, between the many things other than Christ and Christ Himself. You may have many things, yet you may not have Christ.

Concerning this matter, I can never forget the help I received from Brother Watchman Nee about thirty years ago. One day he spoke with me, saying, "Brother Lee, when I was very young, a little more than twenty years of age, I was under the help of an elderly sister, Miss M. E. Barber. Many times when famous preachers with prominent titles came to our town, Miss Barber would bring me with her, and at other times I would ask her to go with me to listen to these world-famous preachers. The first time we went, in my heart I truly appreciated the preacher. I felt that he was very eloquent, smart, and knowledgeable, and I truly admired him. Then the next day when I sat with Miss Barber in her living room, she asked me what I thought about the preacher the previous night. I said, 'He is wonderful!' She went on to ask, 'Wonderful in what?' I said, 'He is surely wonderful in knowledge, in ability, in eloquence, and so forth.' Then she asked, 'What is that? Is that something which is Christ Himself? Is that something that comes out of the inner fellowship? Can you realize that the speaker is really one who is in fellowship with Christ?'" Brother Nee told me that after being asked in that way, he simply had nothing to say except one word, no. Was that something which is Christ Himself? No. Was that something from the inner fellowship? No. Was that speaker in fellowship with Christ? No.

After a certain time another speaker came. This one was more famous than all the ones who had come before. Brother Nee went to Miss Barber and asked her to go with him to listen to that big speaker. While they were listening, Brother Nee was really happy and said within himself, "O Miss Barber, this time you have to be convinced. Here is something really bigger and better." After they came back, Brother Nee had no patience to wait until the next day. He right away asked her, "What about this one?" Miss Barber calmly asked him, "Is this one in the fellowship of the Lord?" Brother Nee told me that her question simply made him clear, and he had to answer, "No." Since that time I have been greatly helped. I may speak very well and I may preach richly, yet there is the possibility that I am not in the fellowship of the Lord. That kind of preaching is a preaching of gift, not a preaching of Christ Himself. Anything that is of Christ, even as Christ Himself, must be in the fellowship of Christ. You must be in the fellowship of Christ. You must have a living contact with Christ.

THE DANGER OF GIFTS, KNOWLEDGE, AND SPIRITUALITY

Brothers and sisters, we need to realize that not only are the gifts something other than Christ and not Christ Himself, but even the knowledge and the teaching of Christ are not Christ Himself. We have to know Christ in a living way, and we have to minister Christ in a real and living way, not merely in the way of knowledge nor in the way of teaching. When you are speaking about Christ, people must be able to sense the presence of Christ. Something from Christ, something out of Christ, even something as Christ must be ministered through you to others. This is the ministry of Christ that is adequate to build up the Body of Christ.

All the gifts are for the building of the church. We have to realize, however, that any gift that is separated from Christ and remains merely a gift is dangerous. It is a damage to the building of the church. I say again, a gift must be for the building of the church, and this gift must be related to Christ. Once a gift is separated from Christ, you may do many things, but this gift will be a damage to the building up of the Body. I do look to the Lord that He would open our eyes to see the difference between the gifts and Christ and between the knowledge of Christ and Christ Himself. Christ Himself is the only factor, the only element, for us to build up the church.

In the past we have seen many things that caused us great sorrow because we have seen a number of gifted people do a great deal of damage to the building up of the Body. The more they work, the more they do, the more they preach, and the more they teach, the more they damage the building of the church. Even the teaching and doctrine concerning Christ can be a dividing factor in the church if you are not in Christ, if you are not exercising your gift by being joined to Christ. By this we can see that there is a real danger with the gifted ones.

From the past to the present time I have noticed that there are some believers who claim to be spiritual. However, I have discovered that the more they claim to be spiritual, the more they cannot be built up with others, and all they can do is simply criticize others all the time. They often say, "I am spiritual, but you are not. I have seen the heavenly vision, but you have not." I am not imagining this; from the Far East to Europe and America, I have met this kind of person everywhere. They have a so-called spirituality which is not Christ Himself; they do not have the real spirituality which is Christ Himself. Hence, wherever I have met them, the impression I have had is that they are always criticizing others. Wherever they go, they consider themselves to be the best. This is a real damage to the Body. This is why recently when I was in a certain locality, I spoke with the dear brothers there, saying, "Let us be general and not special. Do not think you are spiritual. If you think you are spiritual, it simply means you are not spiritual. If you claim that you have seen the heavenly vision, it simply means that what you have seen is an earthly vision. When you claim that you are spiritual, you have to know that you are fleshy and carnal. When the heavenly light was on the face of Moses, Moses did not see it. It was others who saw it. To be truly spiritual is to be humble and general toward others."

Brothers and sisters, gifts are not Christ. Knowledge and teachings are not Christ. Even so-called spirituality is not Christ. Only Christ Himself is Christ. You must forget about the gifts you have, the knowledge and teachings you have obtained, and the so-called spirituality to which you have attained. You have to forget about all these things. Simply keep yourself in a living communion with the living Lord. Contact Him in a humble way, saying, "Lord, I am nothing. I am not better than anyone. Nothing with me is special. I am very general. I am just a sinner saved by You, and that is all." Let others discern whether or not we are spiritual.

We need to realize who Christ is. Christ is the One who is simply experienced by us in a living way. I do not mean that we do not need certain kinds of gifts. I do not mean that we do not need knowledge and teachings. We need these things, but we have to realize that they must not be something other than Christ. Only Christ Himself avails for the building up of the church. Therefore, let us be humble to experience Christ. Let us be humble all the time in teaching the real experience of Christ. He is the living Lord. Now He is the living Spirit, and He is embodied in the living Word. We need to humbly contact the Word in the spirit to experience the living Lord Himself. If you will do this, I am sure you will have a desire for the church life, and you will experience Christ in a real and living way. You will long to have the church life, you will be desirous to be built up together with others, and you will love others. Furthermore, you will never consider yourself special. Rather, you will be very general.

If any one among us still considers himself or herself as someone special, this is a damage to the building up of the Body. If you still consider yourself as someone special, you will have nothing but criticism in your heart. You will be criticizing all the time. You may say in your heart, "This brother's message this morning is good" or "The meetings in these days are not bad," but you will have something further critical to say. You will always criticize something. This simply proves that you consider yourself as someone superior to others, someone better than others, someone special. I beg you, if you do have the desire to build up the Lord's Body in a practical way in your locality, give up this kind of thought. Simply be very general and simple.

All the so-called spiritual persons are too complicated. Forgive me to say this; I hope that I am saying this in love. In recent years I have considered giving up my pursuit to be "spiritual." I do not want to be "spiritual," because to be "spiritual" simply means to be complicated. The most complicated people are the spiritual ones. When I am not spiritual, I am very simple and I love the brothers, but when I become spiritual, immediately I become complicated and begin to ask, "Is this brother spiritual? Has he seen the heavenly vision?" This is why I say that in recent years I have been afraid to be "spiritual." I have been nearly quenched by "spiritual" people. Most of the problems and difficulties that come into the church are from those who claim to be spiritual, not from those who are not spiritual. The more someone claims to be spiritual, the more problems and difficulties he brings into the church. In the Far East we did not have any problem before we had certain "spiritual" persons. Only a few years ago, when a small number of people became "spiritual," the trouble came. I say again, I am afraid to be "spiritual," and I am afraid to see you being "spiritual."

What I mean is that there is nothing besides Christ that is good for the building up of the church. Do not pay much attention to the so-called gifts, to mere teachings and knowledge, or to so-called spirituality. Forget about all these things. Be humble to contact the living Lord day by day and to be general and simple. Do not try to analyze people. The "spiritual" people are the best, expert analyzers. They are analyzing all the time. Brothers and sisters, try to be simple and not to be clever. If we are simple, we will love the brothers, and we will not like to analyze them. It is love in Christ that builds. Knowledge does not build but puffs up.

Gifts, knowledge, teachings, spirituality, and even spiritual experiences are not Christ. Only Christ Himself is Christ. You have to experience Christ day by day and even moment by moment. Contact Him. If you have a living contact with Christ today, you will not be proud and you will not criticize others. I do desire to see that in these days and in this country a good number of believers would love the Lord, contact Him, and live by Him in a real and living way. We may never talk about gifts, yet we may have many gifts. We may never talk about knowledge, yet we may have profound spiritual knowledge. Likewise, we may not talk about our "spiritual" experiences, but we simply contact the living Lord day by day and live by Him. We will simply speak about Christ in love and in humility. We will love all the saints and all kinds of saints. This is the life that can build up the church, and this is the life that can cover all the shortcomings. Moreover, this life is love and light. May the Lord deliver us not only from sins, from fleshly things, and from worldly things but also from gifts, knowledge, and "spiritual" experiences.

CHRIST VERSUS THE LAW

The apostle Paul told the Galatians that it was God's pleasure to reveal His Son in him (Gal. 1:15-16), and he told them that Christ would be formed in them (4:19). This was because at that time the Galatian believers were very much influenced by the teaching of the law, the teaching to keep the law (3:2, 5). The law is something from God. It is good, holy, divine, righteous, spiritual, and perfect (Rom. 7:12-14). However, the law is not Christ. We are not bound to the law at all. We are simply bound to Christ. Christ, not the law, is the central thought of God. The law is not the center, but Christ is. So the apostle told the Galatians how he used to be under the law, but one day God revealed His Son in him. That was something other than the law. From that time on he could discern the difference between the law and Christ, and he gave up the law and kept Christ. He told the Galatians that today with us, the Christians, it is not a matter of keeping the law but a matter of living by Christ. He said, "I am crucified with Christ; and it is no longer I who live, but it is Christ who lives in me" (Gal. 2:20). He also said, "I through the law have died to the law" (v. 19). He had nothing to do with the law. He was a dead person to the law. As far as the law was concerned, he was dead and finished. He was bound to Christ, and it was Christ who lived in him.

Strictly speaking, no one is teaching the law today, but you have to realize that many times you yourself are like a teacher of the law. Perhaps every morning in your prayer you are a good teacher trying your best to teach yourself to do good. You are the law teacher and the law giver to yourself, and you yourself even become the law. You may set up many laws for yourself to do good. You may set up a law to sacrifice for the Lord and a law to be humble, to love others, and to help others. You may have more laws than the Ten Commandments, and you may be a better law giver than Moses. Do you realize that you have been very much influenced by trying to do good? You must forget about trying to do good. We are not bound to do good. We are bound to Christ. Can you forget about doing good? If you are still trying to do good, you are a "Galatian."

CHRIST VERSUS RELIGION

Not only so, but there is also the case of the Hebrew believers. Hebrews 1:2 says that God "has at the last of these days spoken to us in the Son," indicating that the Son, Christ, is the center, the focus, of this book. The Hebrew believers held on to a sound, fundamental, good, and even genuine religion—Judaism, which may even be considered a religion from God and from the heavens. However, it is not Christ. Today we are not bound to any kind of religion, not even to Christianity. Inasmuch as Christianity is a religion, we have nothing to do with it. Christianity is not Christ Himself. Often I tell people that there are the words *Christ* and *Christian* in the Scriptures, but there is not the word *Christianity*. *Christianity* is a human-manufactured word, and I do not like to use it. Christianity is a dead religion, a religion other than Christ.

In the Epistle to the Hebrews there is a big difference between Christ and all the good things of the genuine, fundamental religion. In that religion there were the angels, the apostles such as Moses and Joshua, and the priests, including the high priest. Furthermore, there were the Scriptures and the temple, including the Holy of Holies, the sacrifices, and the rituals. All the good, sound, fundamental, and genuine things of religion were there, yet all these are not Christ Himself. Anything that is not Christ Himself is not good for the building up of the Body of Christ. The building up of the Body of Christ must be something which is Christ Himself. We have to know Christ in a living way. We have to experience Christ in a real way. Christ must be everything. He is the real Angel from God. He is the real Apostle from God. He is the real Priest, the High Priest. He is the temple and the sacrifices. Christ is everything.

What is the church? The church is Christ. It is not a "New Testament church" but a "Christ church." Today in this country I have learned that many Christians like to use the term "New Testament church." The first time I heard this term, I said to myself, "What is the New Testament church? Is this another category of Christianity?" I do not think this is a proper term for us to use. We should not say that we are going to have a New Testament church. We are not going to have a new movement and form a new church. This is something that cannot please God. There are enough movements in Christianity. There are enough kinds of "churches"; there is no need for us to add another one. What we need to see is that we must experience Christ. Everything must be Christ. Even the church life must be Christ. Even the fellowship among us must be Christ, not a religion nor Christianity, but Christ.

CHRIST VERSUS PHILOSOPHY

Now let us go on to the book of Colossians. The problem with the Colossians was pagan philosophy, the worldly philosophy, Gnosticism. Even today there is the danger that some philosophy, some thoughts of pagan teachings, worldly teachings, and worldly doctrines will be brought into the church. Christ is the real knowledge, wisdom, philosophy, and teaching. Christ is everything. The apostle Paul told us that all the treasures of wisdom and knowledge are hidden in Christ (Col. 2:3) and that Christ is all and in all (3:11).

If you look into the book to the Colossians, you will realize that in the mind of God and in the thought of the apostle there was nothing but Christ, neither gifts, healings, teachings, doctrines, philosophies, nor worldly elements. Christ is life (3:4), and He is in us as the hope of glory (1:27). He is everything to us. Furthermore, this Christ is the very element, the very factor, for the building up of the Body. If we are going to have the real church life, we must realize Christ in such a living way.

CHRIST VERSUS GIFTS AND KNOWLEDGE

We should also consider the first Epistle to the Corinthians. In 1 Corinthians the apostle told the Corinthian believers that they did not lack in any gift (1:7). They were exceedingly rich in gifts. Moreover, they were enriched in Christ in all knowledge (v. 5). However, what the apostle preached was neither gifts nor knowledge but Christ. In 1:22-23 Paul said, "For indeed Jews require signs and Greeks seek wisdom, but we preach Christ crucified." The Jews sought signs, the miraculous things, and the Greeks sought wisdom, knowledge, and philosophy. Today in Christianity, people are still seeking these two categories of things. They are seeking gifts, signs, and miracles, and they also are seeking knowledge and teaching. However, Paul said he preached Christ, who is the power of God and the wisdom of God (v. 24).

I say again, you may have all the gifts, yet you may not have Christ. You may be very rich in gifts yet very poor in Christ. The Corinthian believers did not lack in any gift. Indeed, they were rich and strong in gifts. However, the apostle told them that they were "fleshy" and were "infants in Christ" (3:1). Some have thought that in the first Epistle to the Corinthians the apostle had a positive attitude concerning the gifts and encouraged the believers to seek the gifts. What we see, however, is exactly the opposite. In 1 Corinthians, the apostle's attitude toward the gifts is very negative. Concerning speaking in tongues, the apostle said that "in the church I would rather speak five words with my mind, that I might instruct others also, than ten thousand words in a tongue" (14:19). To be sure, this word is not encouraging but discouraging toward the gifts. At the end of chapter twelve, after speaking a great deal concerning the gifts, he said, "And moreover I show to you a most excellent way" (v. 31). What is the most excellent way? The most excellent way to exercise the gifts is love (ch. 13). If you can speak in the tongues of men and of angels, but do not have love, you are like a sounding brass or a clanging cymbal, in which there is no life and no reality (v. 1). This is surely not an encouraging word concerning the gifts. You may exercise different kinds of gifts and even "play" with the gifts as little children play with their toys, yet you may not have love. I do not believe that the attitude of the apostle here is encouraging. Rather, it is discouraging. The apostle was telling the Corinthians that they needed to know Christ, to grow up, and to exercise their gifts in love. All the gifts have to be controlled by love.

Therefore, the law is not Christ, religion is not Christ, philosophy is not Christ, and even the gifts are not Christ. Christ is something other than these things. These four books—Galatians, Hebrews, Colossians, and 1 Corinthians— were written to deal with all the different things that are not Christ. Galatians deals with the law, Hebrews deals with religion, Colossians deals with philosophy, and 1 Corinthians deals with the gifts and knowledge. Today our burden is for the building up of a living expression of the Body of Christ. We must realize that, if we are going to have the real church life, we must forget about all the different kinds of good things that are other than Christ Himself. No matter what kind of good things we pay attention to, as long as they are not Christ, they will be a damage. All things must be related to Christ and must be for Christ. Otherwise, we need to forget about them. The unique way for us to realize the real church life is to experience Christ in a living way. Only Christ will not make us proud. All the other good things, even the so-called spiritual experiences, will make us proud, and that will be a damage to the building up of the church. Only Christ Himself will make us humble, general, and simple, so that it will be easy to build up the church. When we are living in Christ, we are simply in the church life.

Chapter Nine

CHRIST AS THE EXPRESSION OF GOD
IN THE CHURCH

Scripture Reading: Col. 2:2; 1:27; Eph. 3:4; 5:32; 1:22-23;
1 Tim. 3:15-16

As we have seen, the central thought of God is Christ with the church. The entire Scriptures with sixty-six books is centered on Christ as the expression of God through the church as His corporate Body.

CHRIST AND THE CHURCH
AS THE TABERNACLE AND TEMPLE OF GOD

In the Old Testament the history of the people of Israel was simply a history of the tabernacle and the temple. In the wilderness, there were about six hundred thousand men between the ages of twenty and fifty who could go to war to fight for God. If each one of them had a wife, this number would have been doubled, and if each couple had children, their number would have more than tripled. Therefore, there may have been more than two million people in the wilderness traveling and doing nothing but handling the tabernacle day by day, day in and day out, for forty years. When they journeyed, they carried the tabernacle with them, and when they stopped, they set up the tabernacle. In the New Testament the principle is the same. Do you know what we Christians are doing all day long? All we should do is handle the tabernacle, which is a type of the increase of Christ, that is, Christ with the church. This is our business. This is our life and our daily living.

Later, after the children of Israel entered into Canaan, they commenced the second part of their history, the history of the temple. When they enjoyed the produce of the land, they were able to bring forth the temple, which was something more solid and more stable than the tabernacle. The temple was the meaning, the explanation, and the center of their life. Likewise, today when we enjoy Christ as the all-inclusive good land, we also are able to bring forth something as the increase of Christ, the enlargement of Christ, that is, the church.

In the New Testament, we are told that "the Word became flesh and tabernacled among us" (John 1:14). This means that Christ Himself, by being incarnated, became the tabernacle, the dwelling place, of God. Then, in John 2:18-21 the Lord Himself told us that His body was the temple of God which the Jewish people were going to destroy. He said, "Destroy this temple, and in three days I will raise it up" (v. 19). The body which the Lord raised up in three days was a much bigger body, an increased body. The Lord's body in the flesh was put to death on the cross, but a mysterious Body was raised up through the resurrection of Christ. This mysterious Body is Christ with all the believers. Christ, including all the believers, is a mysterious temple for God. So, in the New Testament, we have Christ as the center and the church as His increase, expansion, and enlargement. In other words, Christ is the Head and the church is the Body. This is the central thought of the entire New Testament.

CHRIST AS THE HEAD AND THE CHURCH AS THE BODY IN THE NEW TESTAMENT

The Universal, Great Man in the Gospels and the Acts

The New Testament reveals to us a great, mysterious, and universal man, with Jesus Christ as the Head and all the believers as the Body. The Gospels, the first four books of the New Testament, reveal to us Christ as the Head; then the Acts reveals the Body. In Acts, we see Christ acting, living, moving, and working in His Body. Some people refer to Acts as the acts of the apostles, but strictly speaking, Acts is the acts of Christ as the Spirit through the apostles, and not only through the apostles but also through all the disciples, through all the believers, through the whole Body. Hence, Acts is the acts of the Head as the Spirit through the Body. Thus, we see the universal, great man—the Head with the Body.

When Saul, who strongly opposed the church, was on his way to Damascus, the Lord met him and said to him, "Saul, Saul, why are you persecuting Me?" (9:4). Saul was greatly amazed and said, "Who are You, Lord?" The Lord said, "I am Jesus, whom you persecute" (v. 5). Saul thought that he was persecuting Peter, Stephen, and the other Jesus-followers, who were people on the earth, but he never thought that he was touching anyone in heaven. To his great surprise a voice from heaven told him that He was the One whom Paul was persecuting and that His name was Jesus. What the Lord was saying to Paul was, "When you persecute Peter, you persecute Me. When you persecute the church, you persecute Me, because I am in the church and the church is a part of Me." This "Me" is the universal, great man, with Christ as the Head and the church as the Body.

The Body of Christ and the Body Life in Romans

After the first five books of the New Testament are the Epistles, from Romans to Jude, followed by the seven epistles to the seven churches in the book of Revelation. All these deal with this great mysterious man by giving us the definition, the explanation, of this great man and telling us how the members of this great man come into being. In the book of Romans we are told clearly that originally we were sinners, but one day we were saved and justified, and gradually we are transformed into the living members, the members in reality, the members functioning in the Body. Then, at the end of Romans we see the Body of Christ and the Body life with all the members. This is the central message of the book of Romans. In brief, Romans reveals to us that we all, whether Jews or Gentiles, were formerly sinners, but through the redemption, justification, deliverance, and transformation of the Triune God we become the members of the living Body of Christ.

Caring for the Head and the Body
in 1 Corinthians

Following this is 1 Corinthians. The first Epistle to the Corinthians deals with the problem of the gifts. The gifts carried the Corinthian believers away from the center. Gifts can distract us from the central line of God, which is Christ as the Head being life to the Body, and the church as the Body with all the believers as living, functioning members. To experience Christ, to feed on Christ, to live by Christ, and to express Christ in a corporate way is the proper and central line. However, the spiritual gifts, which seemed to be good and of God, distracted the Corinthians from the proper and central line to pay attention to something other than Christ and the church.

Since the Corinthian believers appreciated the gifts, they also appreciated and highly valued the gifted persons. Some appreciated Paul, others appreciated Apollos, and still others appreciated Peter (1:12). They appreciated the gifts and the gifted persons, but they forgot the Giver. Paul was a gift, Apollos was a gift, and Peter was a gift. However, they are not the Giver, they are not the Head, and they are not Christ. The Corinthian believers did not know Christ deeply, and they did not know the church in the way of Christ. They paid too much attention to the gifts rather than to Christ and the church. Hence, the apostle Paul told them, "We preach Christ crucified" (v. 23). Furthermore, he said, "I did not determine to know anything among you except Jesus Christ, and this One crucified" (2:2). The apostle tried his best to bring the distracted believers from the gifts back to Christ and the church.

In 1 Corinthians 11 we have Christ as the Head and the church as the Body. In this chapter, the apostle Paul told us that in the church the believers need to do two things, to properly care for head covering and to have the Lord's supper in a proper way. The real significance of head covering is to respect the headship of Christ. God is the head of Christ, Christ is the head of every man, and the man is the head of the woman (v. 3). Hence, there must be the head covering.

This is not merely a teaching or a custom but a realization and respect of the headship of Christ. As the church, we have to realize the headship of Christ; we have to realize that Christ is the Head.

Verses 17-34 speak of the Lord's supper. Why do we come together around the Lord's table week after week? Is it simply to remember that the Lord died for us? That is too low and shallow. In verse 29 we are told that we need to discern the Body and that we eat and drink judgment to ourselves if we do not discern the Body. We who are many are one bread, one Body (10:17). When we participate in the Lord's table, we must discern whether the bread on the table signifies the one Body of Christ. Thus, in the first part of 1 Corinthians 11 there is the Head, and in the last part there is the Body. All the gifts must be for the expression of Christ and the building up of the Body. Otherwise, the gifts become something that distracts the Lord's people from the central line. No matter how good something is, we have to realize that as long as it is separated from Christ and the Body, it is something wrong and misused. Today even many divine things are misused through human handling so that what should be a help to the building up of the church becomes a damage, a separating element, and a dividing factor.

Transformation in 2 Corinthians

Next let us consider 2 Corinthians. This book mentions nothing about the gifts. What is dealt with in this book is transformation. We have to be transformed day by day from our natural life to the glorious image of the Lord (3:18). Although the outer man is being consumed, the inner man is being renewed (4:16). This is not a matter of gifts but a matter of transformation. We may illustrate transformation with an ugly caterpillar, which after a period of time becomes a beautiful butterfly. It is transformed from something ugly to something beautiful. Today on the one hand, we are a caterpillar, but praise the Lord, on the other hand, we are becoming a butterfly. However, we are not yet formed and beautified, so there is the need of the process of transformation. While this transforming process is going on, if someone tries to add something to us to make us beautiful, that will not help us but will only spoil the process of transformation. I have noticed in the past years that while certain brothers were in the process of transformation, others tried to help them to have the gifts in order to make them beautiful outwardly. They received certain gifts, but their transformation was spoiled. For us Christians, few things are as dangerous as the gifts. Many Christians have been spoiled in the process of their transformation and in their growth of life by the gifts. In many cases, I have worshipped God for not giving gifts to certain ones.

The second Epistle to the Corinthians mentions nothing about the gifts. Instead, it speaks of the experience of the cross through suffering upon suffering, death upon death, and consuming upon consuming. The apostle Paul did not speak much about his gifts; rather, he spoke a great deal about his sufferings. In 4:10-11 he tells us that he was "always bearing about in the body the putting to death of Jesus" and was "always being delivered unto death for Jesus' sake." Day by day our outer man is decaying, being consumed, and our inner man is being renewed. This is transformation. The building up of the church, the real expression of Christ in a corporate way, depends on the transformation from the old man to the new man, from the natural man to the spiritual man, and from the old nature to the new nature.

If we look at the situation of the church today, we have to admit that troubles in the church are often due to having too many gifts. We may need to pray, "Lord, take back all the gifts and grant us the growth of life. Stop all the gifts but encourage transformation in life." We need the transformation of life and in life. The more gifts the Lord's people have, the more troubles, the more divisions, and the more opinions the church will have. This is a fact. For this reason, in 2 Corinthians the experienced apostle forgot about the gifts and gave up all the matters related to the gifts. He told us that we need to be consumed, renewed, and transformed. We need to learn not to get rid of the thorn but to suffer under the thorn in order to know and experience the sufficient grace (12:7-9).

Experiencing Christ as Everything
for the Body in Galatians

Now let us consider Galatians. In the Epistle to the Galatians we see that the believers were distracted from Christ and the church by attempting to keep the law and to do good. As long as you can do good, you will be very independent. Almost all good people are independent. The more you are a good person, the more independent you are. If you can be a humble person, you will be an independent, proud "humble" person. It is only Christ who does not make people proud, while the good we do becomes a factor that makes us proud. If I can be patient, patience becomes a factor to make me proud. I may say, "Oh, I am patient, and you are not!" To say this shows that I am really a proud person. I am afraid of good persons in the church. They are the most difficult ones to deal with. However, this does not mean that bad persons are easy to deal with. Both the good and the bad are not easy to deal with. Today it is only a matter of Christ: Christ revealed in me (1:16), Christ living in me (2:20), Christ being formed in me (4:19), and I having put on Christ (3:27). Everything is Christ, not the law or goodness. If we try to keep the law or try to do good, we can never build up the church. There is only one thing that can build up the church, and that is Christ Himself experienced by us as everything. When we experience Christ as everything, there is the possibility for the building up of the Body.

Holding to Christ for the Body in Ephesians

Now we go on to Ephesians. Ephesians 1:22-23 tells us that the church is the Body of Christ, who is the Head. In 2:21-22 we see that the church is also the temple, the dwelling place, of God. Then in 5:24-25 we are told that the church is the bride, the wife, the counterpart, of Christ. In 5:32 the apostle tells us, "This mystery is great, but I speak with regard to Christ and the church."

We are also told that we have to be very careful. If we are still childish, if we remain as little children, we will be tossed by waves and carried about by every wind of teaching (4:14).

Today in Christianity there are many different winds of teaching blowing all the time to carry people away from Christ the Head and from the truth. Therefore, we must hold to truth (4:15). Truth is God Himself in Christ. To hold to truth is to hold to God, to hold to Christ, and to forget about all the different teachings and doctrines that blow all the time to carry people away from the experience of Christ the Head. Therefore, we have to grow to become a full-grown man and to have the full knowledge of the Son of God. Then we will be one, not in doctrines but in the faith (v. 13). This faith is the faith that saves us. Doctrines, such as the different doctrines concerning rapture, have nothing to do with our salvation. Whether you believe in pre-tribulation, post-tribulation, or partial rapture does not matter for your salvation. As long as you believe that the Lord Jesus is the Son of God incarnated to be a man who died on the cross, resurrected on the third day, and is now the living Lord, you are saved.

Today some people insist on foot-washing, some insist on head covering, and some insist on greeting one another with a holy kiss. All these things become winds of teachings among Christians, blowing them away from Christ. Regardless of whether or not you wash others' feet, as long as you hold to truth, to Christ as the Head, the supply, the center, and the fountain, and as long as you experience Christ in a living way, all other things can be dropped. Do not forget that the church is the Body of Christ, and we are the members of the Body. We need to hold to Christ to keep ourselves in contact with Christ day by day in living fellowship with Him. This will make us the living, functioning, and growing members of the Body. Then we will be the Body to express Christ in a corporate way. We will be the habitation, the dwelling place, of God for His satisfaction and rest, and we will be the bride, the counterpart, of Christ.

The Experience of Christ
for the Oneness in Philippians

Next we have the Epistle to the Philippians. Philippians is a book dealing with the experience of Christ in different circumstances—in sufferings, in hardships, and in all kinds of persecutions. We can experience Christ in any environment, and if we do, we will keep the oneness of the church. Christ experienced by us is the oneness of the church. We are one in Christ, not in opinions, thoughts, or teachings. If we love the Lord and give up all other things, even the best gifts and teachings, and if we simply contact the Lord and experience Him as everything, we will realize the real oneness among the children of God. The real church life depends only upon the experience of Christ. Among the Philippian believers there were differences of opinions and thinking, so the apostle told them that they needed to experience Christ, to have Christ as their pattern (2:5-11), and to pursue Christ as their goal and gain Him as their prize (3:12-14). If we experience Christ, seek Christ, and follow Christ, we will be one with others. Christ Himself experienced by us is the oneness among the believers.

Christ as Everything to Us in Colossians

Following Philippians, we have the Epistle to the Colossians. Colossians is a short yet wonderful book, a book full of Christ, revealing Christ as everything. Christ is the image of God (1:15a). Christ is the embodiment of God, the One in whom God's fullness dwells (1:19; 2:9). Christ is the Firstborn of all creation, the Head of the church, and the Firstborn from the dead. As such, He must have the first place, that is, the preeminence, in all things (1:15b, 18). Christ is the mystery of God (2:2). Furthermore, Christ is our food, our drink, and our feast, and Christ is the new moon and the Sabbath (2:16). Christ is the reality of all positive things as shadows (v. 17). Christ is all and in all in the church, the Body, the new man (3:10-11). Christ is our life (v. 4), and Christ in us is the hope of glory (1:27). Hence, Christ is everything to us.

Christ as Our Hope in 1 and 2 Thessalonians

Next, we come to the two Epistles to the Thessalonians. First and 2 Thessalonians deal with Christ as hope to us. We are waiting for the coming of our Lord Jesus (1 Thes. 1:3; 2:19; 4:13; 5:8; 2 Thes. 2:16). Christ is our only hope. We have no hope other than Christ.

Our Walk in the Church
in 1 Timothy through Philemon

Then we have four books—1 and 2 Timothy, Titus, and Philemon—which form one group. This group of four books deals with our walk in the church while the Lord delays His coming. In 1 Timothy 3:15 Paul said, "If I delay, I write that you may know how one ought to conduct himself in the house of God, which is the church of the living God, the pillar and base of the truth." This means that while the Lord is tarrying, while He delays His coming back, we know how to conduct ourselves in the house of God, the church of the living God. Furthermore, this very church is the great mystery of God manifested in the flesh (v. 16), not only in the flesh of One, but in the flesh of thousands. When Christ was in the flesh, He was one flesh. Now all the members of His Body are also flesh. God was manifested in the flesh of Jesus, and today God is manifested in the flesh of all the believers. This is a great mystery. On the one hand, the church is the house of God, the dwelling place of God, the place for His rest and satisfaction. On the other hand, the church is the pillar, the supporting power, and the base, the foundation, of the reality, which is God Himself. The church is also a mystery to express God in human nature. We need to know how to conduct ourselves in such a church, how to be elders, how to be deacons and deaconesses, and how to simply love others, as Paul instructed Philemon to love Onesimus, his runaway slave who became a brother in Christ.

The All-inclusive, Living Christ in Hebrews

Now we come to the book to the Hebrews. This book is very glorious. It deals with the difference between the all-inclusive, living Christ and a genuine, sound, fundamental, yet dead religion. We do not have a religion, not even a Christian religion, Christianity. What we have is a living Christ, a living person. What we need is not a religion in knowledge, teaching, or letters, but a living person, that is, the living Son of the living God. He is everything. He is all in all to us.

The Proper Works, the Divine Government, the Divine Fellowship, and the Faith in James through Jude

Following Hebrews, we have the letter written by James to reconcile the real faith with proper works. Then the two letters written by Peter deal with the divine government to rule all things for Christ, so that all things may work together for the good of the Body of Christ, the spiritual building of God. After the two Epistles of Peter we have the three Epistles written by John that deal with the divine fellowship, the fellowship of the Father with the Son. Then we have the book of Jude that deals with heresies and apostasy.

The Local Expressions of Christ and the Ultimate Consummation in Revelation

Finally, in the book of Revelation, we have the seven epistles revealing to us that the churches are the local expressions of Christ in a corporate way (chs. 2—3). Every local church is a lampstand, a testimony, a local expression of the Body to express Christ in a corporate way. Then, eventually, at the end of the book of Revelation, which is also the end of the writings of John, of the New Testament, and of all the Scriptures, we have the greatest, unique, universal lampstand— the New Jerusalem, the holy city—as the all-inclusive, universal, and greatest testimony and expression of God in Christ (chs. 21—22). So, in the book of Revelation we have the seven local lampstands at the beginning and the unique, universal lampstand at the end. All the lampstands are made of pure gold. The holy city is of pure gold, and the throne of God in Christ is at the peak of that city, just as a lamp is on the top of a lampstand. This is the ultimate consummation, the ultimate issue, the ultimate conclusion, of all the Scriptures.

Now we can see what the central thought of God is, and we can see what the very thing is that we should seek after and be in, that is, Christ with the church. Hence, we must forget everything except Christ and the church. We must have the sincere desire to experience Christ in a full way so that His

Body may be built up as a corporate expression wherever we are. May the Lord be gracious to us.

CHAPTER TEN

THE PICTURE OF GOD'S DIVINE BUILDING— THE NEW JERUSALEM

Scripture Reading: Rev. 21; 22:1-2

THE NEW HEAVEN AND THE NEW EARTH WITH THE NEW JERUSALEM

Revelation 21:1 says, "And I saw a new heaven and a new earth; for the first heaven and the first earth passed away, and the sea is no more." The main items in the old creation are the heaven, the earth, and the sea. However, in the new creation, there are only the heavens and the earth, while the sea is no more. The sea has been done away with. Verse 2 says, "And I saw the holy city, New Jerusalem, coming down out of heaven from God, prepared as a bride adorned for her husband." The New Jerusalem is something of heaven but does not remain in heaven. It comes down from God out of heaven, out of the place where God is. Furthermore, the New Jerusalem, the holy city, is a bride adorned for her husband. She is a city, yet she is a bride and she has a husband.

Verse 3 says, "And I heard a loud voice out of the throne, saying, Behold, the tabernacle of God is with men, and He will tabernacle with them, and they will be His peoples, and God Himself will be with them and be their God." This city is, on the one hand, a bride, and on the other hand, a tabernacle. In this verse the Greek word rendered *tabernacle* is used twice, once as a noun and once as a verb. This city is the tabernacle of God through which and within which God tabernacles with man. John 1:14 says, "And the Word became flesh and tabernacled among us (and we beheld His glory, glory as of the only Begotten from the Father), full of grace and reality." When the

Lord, who is the Word, became flesh, He tabernacled among us. The Lord's human body was a tabernacle in which He tabernacled among the human race. Now the New Jerusalem, the holy city, in principle is exactly the same. It is the tabernacle of God through which God tabernacles with man.

Revelation 21:4-5 says, "And He will wipe away every tear from their eyes; and death will be no more, nor will there be sorrow or crying or pain anymore; for the former things have passed away. And He who sits on the throne said, Behold, I make all things new. And He said, Write, for these words are faithful and true." As we have seen, there are two creations of God in the universe. The first is the old creation, and the second is the new creation. Here we are told that all things of the old creation have passed away and God has made all things new. In the new creation there is a new heaven, a new earth, and the New Jerusalem. Everything is new. We must remember what the difference between the new creation and the old creation is. The old creation has nothing of God mingled with it, whereas the new creation does have God mingled with it. The old creation was created as an empty vessel, an empty container, with man as the center with a mouth to take in God, so that God might be mingled with man. Therefore, the old creation is an empty vessel without God mingled with it, but the new creation is a new vessel with God contained in it and mingled with it.

Verses 6-8 say, "And He said to me, They have come to pass. I am the Alpha and the Omega, the Beginning and the End. I will give to him who thirsts from the spring of the water of life freely. He who overcomes will inherit these things, and I will be God to him, and he will be a son to Me. But the cowardly and unbelieving and abominable and murderers and fornicators and sorcerers and idolaters and all the false, their part will be in the lake which burns with fire and brimstone, which is the second death."

THE NEW JERUSALEM

The Bride, the Wife of the Lamb

Verse 9 says, "And one of the seven angels who had the seven bowls full of the seven last plagues came and spoke with me, saying, Come here; I will show you the bride, the wife of the Lamb." In these verses we are told clearly that in the new creation, the new universe, there will be a bride, and this bride is the wife of the Lamb. The New Jerusalem is the bride, the wife, the counterpart, of the Lamb, who is the Son of God, the Lord Christ. What is the difference between the bride and the wife? The bride is for the wedding day, but after the wedding day, the bride becomes the wife. At the beginning of the coming age the New Jerusalem will be the bride, but after that, the New Jerusalem will be the wife of the Lamb.

The Holy City

Verse 10 says, "And he carried me away in spirit onto a great and high mountain and showed me the holy city, Jerusalem, coming down out of heaven from God." In verses 2 and 10, several words are used to describe this city. It is a new city, and it is a holy city. The New Jerusalem is something new, and it is something holy, something separated from all other things unto God to match God. Moreover, it is something great, not small.

Her Glory and Appearance

Verse 11 continues, "Having the glory of God. Her light was like a most precious stone, like a jasper stone, as clear as crystal." The new city, the New Jerusalem, has the glory of God. This simply means that the God of glory shines through her. Her light is like a most precious stone, like a jasper stone. In the figures and types of the Scriptures, what does jasper represent? The explanation is in chapter four, where verses 2-3a say, "Immediately I was in spirit; and behold, there was a throne set in heaven, and upon the throne there was One sitting; and He who was sitting was like a jasper stone." The One on the throne, who is the Lord God Himself, has the appearance of a jasper stone. Thus, jasper stands for the appearance, likeness, and expression of God. The New Jerusalem, the holy city, has the glory of God, and her light is like a jasper stone, having the appearance, likeness, and expression of God. Her appearance, her shining likeness, is exactly the same as the appearance and likeness of God. Therefore, the holy city, the New Jerusalem, is the expression of God. God is expressed through her, and her expression, appearance, and likeness is nothing but God Himself. Therefore, her light is like jasper, shining continually as God does.

Her Structure and Measurement

The Wall, Gates, and Foundations of the City

Verse 12 in chapter twenty-one says, "It had a great and high wall and had twelve gates, and at the gates twelve angels, and names inscribed, which are the names of the twelve tribes of the sons of Israel." The wall of the city is great and high, not small and low. This wall has twelve gates, and on the twelve gates are inscribed the twelve names of the twelve tribes of Israel. This means that the Israelites are the entrances, the gates, into the holy city, implying that the gospel is out of the Jews. It is the Jewish nation, the people of Israel, who began to preach the gospel from Jerusalem to the uttermost part of the earth to bring people to share and enter into the holy city. Verse 13 says, "On the east three gates, and on the north three gates, and on the south three gates, and on the west three gates." There are three gates on each of the four sides, comprising the number twelve, which is composed of three times four.

Verse 14 says, "And the wall of the city had twelve foundations, and on them the twelve names of the twelve apostles of the Lamb." The foundations are also twelve in number, and on the twelve foundations are the names of the twelve apostles. The holy city having twelve gates (the twelve tribes) and twelve foundations (the twelve apostles) clearly indicates that the New Jerusalem is a composition of two groups of people, the Old Testament saints represented by the twelve tribes and the New Testament saints represented by the twelve apostles of Christ.

The Measurements of the City

Verses 15-16 say, "And he who spoke with me had a golden reed as a measure that he might measure the city and its gates and its wall. And the city lies square, and its length is as great as the breadth. And he measured the city with the reed to a length of twelve thousand stadia; the length and the breadth and the height of it are equal." The measurements of the city are composed of the number twelve. The gates are twelve, the foundations are twelve, and the measurement of each dimension of the city is also twelve, but here it is one thousand times twelve. The length is twelve thousand stadia, the width is twelve thousand stadia, and the height is twelve thousand stadia. The city is a cube, that is, it has four sides in three dimensions, once again producing the number twelve. Creation extends in four directions, and the four sides of the New Jerusalem are toward the four directions of the whole universe. Moreover, the three dimensions—length, breadth, and height—imply the Divine Trinity. In the number twelve, four represents the creatures, as with the four living creatures in 4:6-9 and 19:4, and three represents the Divine Trinity, the Triune God. When the Triune God mingles with the creatures, we have twelve, signifying completion in administration. When God, represented by three, is mingled with man, represented by four, we have eternal completion and the eternal government, the eternal administration, represented by twelve.

Verse 17 says, "And he measured its wall, a hundred and forty-four cubits, according to the measure of a man, that is, of an angel." One hundred forty-four is twelve times twelve, signifying the completion of completions. What then is the meaning of the measure of a man being the measure of an angel? Do not forget that all the things recorded in this chapter are signs. Man is the center of the living things on this earth and the angels are the center of all the things created by God in the heavens. The measurement of a man being the measurement of an angel means that with the holy city, the New Jerusalem, heaven and earth are mingled together. Today there is a difference between heaven and earth and between angels and human beings. One day, however, when the New Jerusalem comes, heaven will be joined with earth, and the things in heaven will be mingled with the things on earth. When that day comes, there will be no more difference between the things in heaven and the things on earth. This very city, this new city, this holy Jerusalem, is the embodiment of the mingling of the things in heaven with the things on the earth. The universe includes time and space. It is a composition of the saints in the Old Testament time and the saints in the New Testament time, and it is also a mingling of the things in heaven and the things on earth. As far as time is concerned, the New Jerusalem is a combination; as far as space is concerned, the New Jerusalem is a mingling. The New Jerusalem is the central item of the whole universe, the center of time and space. In her, the Old Testament saints and the New Testament saints are combined, and the things in the heavens and the things on the earth are mingled as one. However, do not misunderstand; there is still a difference between angels and men, but as far as the mingling of the holy city is concerned, there is no difference between heaven and earth.

The Appearance of the City

Verse 18 says, "And the building work of its wall was jasper; and the city was pure gold, like clear glass." Here jasper is mentioned again. The appearance of the city is like the shining of jasper, and the whole wall is made of jasper. The city itself is gold, while the wall built upon it is jasper. When you look at the city from a distance, you do not see the gold. What you see is its jasper wall, for the whole appearance of the city is jasper. As we have seen, jasper stands for the appearance of God. Hence, the city is in the nature of God as gold, and the wall is in the appearance of God as jasper. The young people who are believers in Christ have God within them as the divine nature, the new nature, signified by the gold. I am sure that they have the divine gold within them, but I am afraid that many are barren gold with little of the shining jasper as the appearance of God built upon them. They have the gold, the divine nature of God, within them by regeneration, because when we are regenerated, we receive God as the golden nature. However, after regeneration we need to be built up by transformation to have something of the appearance of God shining as jasper. When you go to certain churches, you can realize that there is something built up that is shining all the time, something that is always attractive. The whole wall of the city is jasper. This means the whole appearance of the city bears the appearance, the likeness, of God. God appears as jasper, and this city also appears as jasper. So, this city has the appearance, the likeness, of God expressed through her.

The Precious Stones
in the Foundations of the Wall

Verses 19-20 say, "The foundations of the wall of the city were adorned with every precious stone: the first foundation was jasper; the second, sapphire; the third, chalcedony; the fourth, emerald; the fifth, sardonyx; the sixth, sardius; the seventh, chrysolite; the eighth, beryl; the ninth, topaz; the tenth, chrysoprase; the eleventh, jacinth; the twelfth, amethyst." The entire wall is jasper with twelve foundations, and all twelve foundations are precious stones. The first stone of the foundation is jasper, which is the same as the wall. If we consider carefully, we can see that the twelve stones are laid upon each other in layers. The twelve layers of precious stones as the foundation in their respective colors have the appearance of a rainbow. Verse 3 of chapter four says, "He who was sitting was like a jasper stone and a sardius in appearance, and there was a rainbow around the throne like an emerald in appearance." The appearance of God in the universe is that of jasper with a rainbow around Him. When the New Jerusalem comes, there is the same picture—a city of jasper with a rainbow. Its appearance is exactly the same as the appearance of God.

The spiritual meaning of a rainbow is seen in Genesis 9:13-17, which says, "I do set my bow in the cloud, and it shall be for a token of a covenant between me and the earth. And it shall come to pass, when I bring a cloud over the earth, that the bow shall be seen in the cloud: and I will remember my covenant, which is between me and you and every living creature of all flesh; and the waters shall no more become a flood to destroy all flesh. And the bow shall be in the cloud; and I will look upon it, that I may remember the everlasting covenant between God and every living creature of all flesh that is upon the earth. And God said unto Noah, This is the token of the covenant, which I have established between me and all flesh that is upon the earth." The rainbow is a token of the everlasting covenant that God will never destroy His living creatures. Hence, the rainbow is a sign of God being the God of covenant, the God of faithfulness, who is faithful to keep the everlasting covenant. That the foundation of this city is a rainbow means that the city is built upon the faithfulness of God. It is a city that can never be destroyed because it is a city of the everlasting covenant of God. The New Jerusalem is a city which has the foundations (Heb. 11:10), and the foundations are the faithfulness of God, the everlasting covenant of God. The foundation of this city is like a rainbow which reminds us and God that we are safe, that we have eternal security. The city in which we will dwell is a city with a rainbow as the foundation to remind God that it is not lawful for Him to destroy it. He is not allowed to destroy it, and He is bound by His everlasting covenant not to destroy it.

The Precious Materials of the City

Revelation 21:21 says, "And the twelve gates were twelve pearls; each one of the gates was, respectively, of one pearl. And the street of the city was pure gold, like transparent glass." Each of the twelve gates is a great pearl. Here we see three kinds of materials: The city itself is gold, the wall upon it is jasper with different kinds of precious stones as the foundation, and the gates are pearls. As we have seen, these three items are in Genesis 2. There are not two or four kinds of materials, but three, signifying the three persons of the Triune God. The gold, signifying the divine nature, is something of God the Father; the pearl, which forms the entrance, is something of God the Son; and the wall with its appearance is something of God the Spirit. This signifies that the Triune God is mingled with and constitutes all the saved ones.

The city itself is gold, and the street of the city, which is one, not many, is also gold. The wall built upon the foundation is of precious stones, and the gates are twelve pearls. Therefore, there is gold, pearl, and precious stones. Gold is the first item. When building the wall of a house, you first must leave a space for the entrance; in this sense, the entrance is first and the wall is built around it. Therefore, the second item is the pearls, and the precious stones are third. This is the order of the materials according to the teaching of the apostle Paul. Paul told us that we should build the church with gold, silver, and precious stones (1 Cor. 3:12), and silver signifies the same thing as pearls. Therefore, in Genesis 2 there are three items, in Revelation 21 there are three items, and in 1 Corinthians 3 there are also three items. All three items are for the building up of the dwelling place of God. These three items signify something of God the Father, God the Son, and God the Spirit. The Triune God is mingled with us and wrought into us. In this way, we have the divine building.

The Enlarged Temple

Revelation 21:22 says, "And I saw no temple in it, for the Lord God the Almighty and the Lamb are its temple." This verse speaks of the temple, but it is different from the temple in the old Jerusalem. With the old Jerusalem, there was the city and there was the temple within the city, but the New Jerusalem is a city in which no temple is seen. Since God Himself in Christ is the divine temple, there is no need of another temple. With this city are both the tabernacle and the temple. As we have seen, the whole Old Testament is a history of the tabernacle and of the temple, and the New Testament is the continued history of the tabernacle and the temple. While the Lord Jesus was on this earth, He tabernacled among men (John 1:14). Furthermore, His body was the temple. This temple, this body, was killed, destroyed, by the Jewish people on the cross, but the Lord raised it up in three days, that is, in resurrection (2:19-21). In resurrection He built up an enlarged temple, which is the church. The ultimate conclusion of all the Scriptures is the city as the tabernacle with the temple. This city is the tabernacle with God in Christ Himself as the temple. Thus again, we have the tabernacle and the temple.

Her Light and Lamp and the Nations around Her

Revelation 21:23 says, "And the city has no need of the sun or of the moon that they should shine in it, for the glory of

God illumined it, and its lamp is the Lamb." God is the light and Christ is the lamp. God is in Christ shining through Christ, just as light is in a lamp and shines through the lamp.

Verses 24-27 speak of the nations, saying, "And the nations will walk by its light; and the kings of the earth bring their glory into it. And its gates shall by no means be shut by day, for there will be no night there. And they will bring the glory and the honor of the nations into it. And anything common and he who makes an abomination and a lie shall by no means enter into it, but only those who are written in the Lamb's book of life."

THE RIVER OF WATER OF LIFE AND THE TREE OF LIFE

Verses 1-2 of chapter twenty-two say, "And he showed me a river of water of life, bright as crystal, proceeding out of the throne of God and of the Lamb in the middle of its street. And on this side and on that side of the river was the tree of life, producing twelve fruits, yielding its fruit each month; and the leaves of the tree are for the healing of the nations." In these verses there are four items, all in singular number: the throne, the river, the street, and the tree. The throne is one, the street is one, the river flowing in the middle of the street is one, and the tree of life growing in the river is also one. In Genesis 2 there is the tree of life with a river flowing beside it, and in Revelation 22 there is again the tree of life with a river constantly flowing. Here is a throne, and from the throne a river flows in the middle of the street. Verse 2 says that "on this side and on that side of the river was the tree of life," indicating that the tree of life is on the two banks of the river. This means that the street is the two banks of the river on which the tree of life grows.

How can one street serve twelve gates, and how can we enter into the city? Remember that the city is very high, twelve thousand stadia in height. The wall, which is also high, though not as high as the city itself, is one hundred forty-four cubits. That the throne is in the center of the city means that the throne must be on the top of the center of the city. By this we can see that the street must be a spiral. From the throne at the top of the city, the street constantly spirals until it reaches to the twelve gates. In this way, all twelve gates use the one street. Because there is only one street, no one can be lost in the city. Regardless of which of the twelve gates you enter, if you proceed on the street, you eventually will reach the throne of God. As long as you enter in, you will know the way on the street. Simply go on continually and you will reach the Lord Jesus.

THE BLESSINGS OF GOD'S REDEEMED IN ETERNITY

Verses 3-7 say, "And there will no longer be a curse. And the throne of God and of the Lamb will be in it, and His slaves will serve Him; and they will see His face, and His name will be on their forehead. And night will be no more; and they have no need of the light of a lamp and of the light of the sun, for the Lord God will shine upon them; and they will reign forever and ever. And he said to me, These words are faithful and true; and the Lord, the God of the spirits of the prophets, has sent His angel to show to His slaves the things which must quickly take place. And behold, I come quickly. Blessed is he who keeps the words of the prophecy of this scroll."

Here, to some extent, we have seen a picture of the holy city. In the next chapters we will continue to see something further.

CHAPTER ELEVEN

THE NEW JERUSALEM
AS GOD'S CORPORATE VESSEL

Scripture Reading: Rev. 21:1-3, 9-14, 16-23; 22:1-2

Students of the Bible realize that the last two chapters of Revelation are the conclusion of the entire Scriptures. In these two chapters we have a picture of a divine building, which is called the holy city, the New Jerusalem, as the conclusion of the entire Scriptures. This conclusion is threefold: It is the conclusion to the writings of the apostle John, which are in the line of life; it is the conclusion to the entire New Testament; and it is the conclusion to the entire Scriptures. By this we can see how important the picture of the New Jerusalem is. Furthermore, as the ultimate conclusion of the entire divine writings, the New Jerusalem is the conclusion of the divine thought.

In the previous chapters we have seen that the central thought of God is to have Christ wrought into a group of people to be life to them and to have them as a corporate expression for Christ so that God may be expressed in Christ through them. In brief, the central thought of God is Christ with a Body to express God. In the last two chapters of Revelation we have a picture that shows us God in Christ on the throne expressed through a corporate vessel—a great and high city. This city is a corporate vessel to contain God in Christ and to express God through Christ. Hence, this picture shows us the central thought of God.

GOD EXPRESSED IN CHRIST
THROUGH THE NEW JERUSALEM

In this record we are told that God at the very center of the city is the light, and the shining of the light is the glory of

God (21:23a). God, who is the light and who is constantly shining, is in the lamp, who is the redeeming Christ, the redeeming Lamb (v. 23b). God is in Christ just as light is in a lamp. That the lamp shines from the center of this great city indicates that every part of the city is transparent. Therefore, the whole city is a corporate vessel, to express God in Christ and through Christ.

I was born, raised, and taught in Christianity. Since I was a little boy I heard many teachings about the New Jerusalem. There were different opinions, different thoughts, and different teachings about this city. When I was young, I simply accepted those teachings. However, by experiencing the Lord in the inner life and in the way of life, and through much study, reading, and deep consideration of all the Scriptures, the Lord gradually revealed to me the right, proper, and adequate explanation and definition of the New Jerusalem. The New Jerusalem is a living, corporate vessel as a container to contain God in Christ and to express God through Christ. We can conclude this because Revelation 21 says that the very God who dwells within this city is the light, and the redeeming One, the Son of God, the Lord Christ as the Lamb, is the lamp. Light shines forth in a lamp to express itself. In this picture of the New Jerusalem, God is the light in the lamp, which is Christ, shining Himself forth in Christ and through Christ. God is one with Christ; we can never separate the light from the lamp. The light is the very essence in the lamp, and it is one with the lamp. The light needs a lamp because it desires to shine forth to express itself. Moreover, the lamp is in the city, which is a corporate vessel, a corporate container. Because this corporate vessel is transparent in every respect and in every part, it is easy for it to shine forth what it contains. The New Jerusalem contains God in Christ and shines forth God through Christ. This is not a mere human thought or my explanation alone. This is the revelation of the divine thought from the divine record.

GOD'S WORK OF BUILDING IN THE NEW CREATION

Here we must review the difference between the old creation of God and His new creation. The old creation was an empty vessel as a container to contain God. It was created by God, but it had nothing of God. The new creation, on the other hand, is the old creation transformed by God by receiving God as its content. The old creation as an empty vessel has no content of God, but the new creation as a corporate vessel is filled with God as its content. Because it is no longer empty but filled with God, it has been transformed from its old shape, form, and nature into a new one. In this way it has become new. Before you were saved, you were an empty vessel, like an empty cup or bottle. You were made by God to contain Him, but you were corrupted and ruined by Satan. Since the time you received the Lord and acknowledged Him as the Redeemer, His blood has cleansed you from all defilement and filth, and at the same time, the Lord has entered into you to fill you up and be your content. Hence, you are no more an empty vessel. Rather, you have become a vessel filled with the Lord. From that time on, due to the filling of the Lord, a change has taken place in you and is still taking place all the time. Do you realize that you are changing day by day, even moment by moment? As an empty vessel, you were the old man and you were a part of the old creation. As a filled vessel with Christ, you are a part of the new man, a part of the new creation.

TWO LINES OF BUILDING IN THE OLD TESTAMENT

After God's work of creation, He began to do a work of building. The new creation is a building work. After God created everything, He began to build up a Body, a corporate vessel, a city, to contain Himself. In the first two chapters of the Bible God finished His work of creation, and from Genesis 3 to the end of the Scriptures what God has been doing has been a building work. God is building Himself and man to be a corporate Body to express Himself. Genesis 3 to the end of the Scriptures is a long record of stage after stage of the building.

Throughout all the Scriptures, the enemy has always tried to discover God's plan and do something before God does. God had an intention to build up a city, but before God did this, the enemy of God did something first. Cain was the second generation of the human race, the first son of Adam. After Cain's separation from God, he built up a city, which he called after the name of his son Enoch (Gen. 4:17). This city of Enoch, built by Cain, became the center of civilization before the flood. All the corruption during that age before the flood was centered in that city. As a sinful city full of sins it was a container of Satan. Therefore, God destroyed that city by the flood. After the flood, God obtained a new world, but something happened again. The descendants of Noah were very much used by the enemy to build up another city, the city of Babel with the tower of Babel (11:4-9). Babel was the original name of Babylon. That was a city of Satan.

In that situation, God called out a person by the name of Abraham (12:1-3). God brought him to an elevated land, signifying the place of resurrection. God put him there and promised him that He would build a city for him. Later on, God did build a city on the elevated land, which was Jerusalem. In the Old Testament, Babylon always opposed Jerusalem. These two cities were always against one another. Eventually, Jerusalem was destroyed by Babylon, and all the utensils for the worship in the temple in Jerusalem were captured and brought by the Babylonians to Babylon and put in the temples of idols there. When Daniel, a faithful servant of God, was captured and remained in Babylon, day by day he opened his windows and looked toward Jerusalem, remembering Jerusalem before God (Dan. 6:10). He never forgot Jerusalem, because he knew the divine thought of God. Later, there was the return of the captives, the recovery, and in that recovery Nehemiah built up the destroyed wall of Jerusalem, which required much fighting (Neh. 4:16-21; 6:15-16).

Earlier, when the people of Israel were enslaved in Egypt, they were forced by the Egyptians to build two cities for Pharaoh with bricks of clay and straw. They had to labor to gather straw and burn the clay into bricks for the building (Exo. 1:11, 14; 5:15-19). This is a picture, typifying that people of God have been captured, kept, and retained under the hand of Satan in the world to labor for Satan in order to build up the world as a container for him. While you are working in the world on your job, you must be careful. Do not do anything to help Pharaoh to build up his two cities as a container to contain Satan and all his corruption. The Lord delivered the children of Israel out of Egypt and brought them through the Red Sea. Then at a certain point the Lord came to them and told them to build a tabernacle for Him, not with straw, mud, clay, or dust, but with gold, silver, and precious stones. That was the building of the tabernacle with the priesthood, full of precious stones and gold, as God's dwelling place. There is a contrast between the building of the cities in Egypt and the building of the tabernacle in the wilderness. The cities built in Egypt were the containers of Satan with all his corruption, while the tabernacle built in the wilderness was a container for God with His holiness.

The foregoing history helps us to understand that the whole Old Testament is a history of building. People were either utilized by Satan, the enemy of God, to build up cities to contain Satan with all his corruption, or they were used by God to build up a city to contain God with His holiness.

TWO LINES OF BUILDING IN THE NEW TESTAMENT

Now we come to the New Testament, which is a further record of building. In Matthew 16 Peter confessed to the Lord, "You are the Christ, the Son of the living God" (v. 16), and the Lord responded, "I also say to you that you are Peter, and upon this rock I will build My church" (v. 18). If we know Christ in a living way, we will realize that we are material for the building of the church. Several times in the New Testament teachings the Lord Jesus is likened to a stone. In Matthew 21:42 the Lord Jesus, quoting from Psalm 118:22-23, indicated to the Jews that He is the cornerstone for God's building. Christ is not only the foundation stone (Isa. 28:16) and the topstone (Zech. 4:7) but also the cornerstone. In his preaching of Christ in Acts 4:11, Peter told the Jews, "This is the stone which was considered as nothing by you, the builders, which has become the head of the corner." This indicates that he preached Christ not only as the Savior for sinners' salvation but also as the stone for God's building.

In the Epistles the apostle Paul speaks much concerning the building. We may say that the teaching of the apostle Paul is a teaching of building. In 1 Corinthians 3:9 he tells us, "We are God's fellow workers; you are...God's building." In the next verse he tells us that he was a wise master builder, the head of a group of workers to build the house of God. Then in verse 12 he tells us that we should build the church with gold, silver, and precious stones. In Ephesians 2:20-21 he tells us that Christ Jesus is the cornerstone "in whom all the building, being fitted together, is growing into a holy temple in the Lord." In 4:12 he speaks of the perfecting of the saints unto the work of the ministry, unto the building up of the Body of Christ.

Peter in his first Epistle also teaches us concerning the building up of the church. He refers to the Lord as "a living stone, rejected by men but with God chosen and precious" (2:4). Then he goes on to say, "You yourselves also, as living stones, are being built up as a spiritual house into a holy priesthood to offer up spiritual sacrifices acceptable to God through Jesus Christ" (v. 5). This indicates that we are God's building to serve God, contain God, and express God.

Then, in the last book of the New Testament we have two great cities. Do not forget that in addition to the New Jerusalem (21:2) there is the city which is called "Mystery, Babylon the Great" (17:5). Here in the last book of the Scriptures Babylon is mentioned again, this time as something against the New Jerusalem. These two cities are two containers. One is the container of Satan to contain Satan with all his corruption, confusion, complications, and divisions. The book of Revelation shows us how much corruption, confusion, complication, and division are contained in this mysterious Babylon, the great Babylon of mystery. That is the building of Satan with humans and among humans. In, among, and with the human race as the material, Satan is building up a mysterious city as a container to contain him and express him. On the other hand, the Lord is building a holy city, the New Jerusalem, among the human race and with the human race as the material to contain God and express God. If we read Revelation, we will see these two cities: the city of Satan and the

city of God, the sinful city and the holy city, the city full of
Satan's corruption and the city full of God's holiness, the city
full of satanic darkness and the city full of God's light, the
city as an incarnation of Satan and the city as an enlarged
incarnation of God. What God is doing today is, on the one
hand, to build up His holy city and, on the other hand, to
destroy the great Babylon of mystery. One day this great city
of Babylon will be fully destroyed. After the destruction of
this great, sinful, satanic city, the time will come for the New
Jerusalem, the holy city, to be manifested.

Do you see the picture in all the Scriptures? It is a record
of building. On the one hand, it is a positive record of the
divine building, and on the other hand, it is a negative record
of the satanic building, the devilish building. In all the
dispensations, generations, and ages, the principle is exactly
the same.

THE NEW JERUSALEM BEING
A LIVING COMPOSITION OF LIVING PERSONS

Now let us see what the New Jerusalem, the divine building, the holy city, is. First, this holy city is a living composition
of living persons. It is built with living persons as materials,
being composed of the saints in the Old Testament time as
well as the saints in the New Testament time. We know that
the New Jerusalem is a composition of living persons because
the divine record tells us that the twelve gates of the city bear
the names of the twelve tribes of Israel (21:12) and that the
twelve foundations of this city bear the names of the twelve
apostles of the Lamb (v. 14). The twelve tribes of Israel are
the representatives of the Old Testament saints, and the
twelve apostles are the representatives of all the New Testament saints. This is why we say that the New Jerusalem is a
composition of all the saints in the Old Testament time as
well as in the New Testament time. From now on you should
never believe that in this universe God is building a material
place with material things. After creating the heavens, the
earth, and all things, God has not had a resting place. God
will not be satisfied with a physical place as His resting
place. In Isaiah 66:1 we are told that even heaven, where

God's throne is, is not God's resting place. What is God's resting place? According to the following verse, it is the contrite
spirit of man. God wants a living dwelling place, that is, a
dwelling place built with living persons.

When I was young, I sat at the feet of some older saints
who taught the Bible in the way of letters. One day I heard a
message saying, "The heavenly mansion which the Lord is
preparing for us must be a wonderful place. The Lord told us
that as soon as He finishes building it, He will come back to
take us there. Since He has been gone for nearly two thousand years and has not come back yet, it must be that the
heavenly mansion has not yet been completed. After such a
long time the Lord still has not finished the building, so imag-
ine how wonderful that mansion will be!" At that time I was
so childish that I believed what I heard, and I even was
excited, thinking that each of us will be given a mansion, as
we sang in certain hymns. This concept concerning the New
Jerusalem is altogether wrong. The Lord is after a living
dwelling place with living persons as living materials.

In Christianity today Christians have a very wrong concept concerning the church. They consider that the church is
a physical building. This is absolutely and seriously wrong.
The church is not a physical building but a building with
living persons. It is a living composition with the living
believers as the living members. The church is not a physical
house; the church is a living house. The same principle
applies to the New Jerusalem. The New Jerusalem is not a
physical building but a living building with living members,
living persons. The Lord does not want to have a physical
mansion as His dwelling place. Rather, the Lord desires to
have a living composition of a living group of living persons,
redeemed, saved, regenerated, transformed, changed in every
respect, and composed and built up together as a living dwelling place for Himself. This is the resting place of the Lord.
This is the highest thought, the thought on the highest plane,
concerning the dwelling place of God.

In certain places some friends asked me, "Brother Lee,
would you please tell us where we Christians will be after we
die?" I said, "Brothers, there is no need for you to worry about

this matter. Surely you and I are precious in the Lord's eyes. The Lord will keep us in the best place." Brothers and sisters, we do not need to worry about where we will be in the future. Rather, the Lord is very concerned today about His spiritual, living dwelling place. He is seeking after a living habitation that is composed of, built up together with, all the redeemed, regenerated, and transformed ones.

The New Jerusalem is the bride of Christ and the wife of Christ (Rev. 21:2, 9). How can a physical mansion be a bride or a wife? When you get married, will you marry a house or a mansion? No, you will marry a living person, a person as a living composition of living members. How can a physical mansion which is without feelings and thoughts match you? In the same way, how can a physical mansion without a heart, a mind, a thought, and a desire be the counterpart to match the living Christ? That is ridiculous. The Lord is going to marry not a physical mansion but His redeemed ones, who are composed together as His bride, His wife.

The apostle John tells us that all the people given by God the Father to the Lord, the Son, are the bride as the increase of the Lord (John 3:29-30). The apostle Paul also says that he betrothed us as pure virgins to Christ as our Husband (2 Cor. 11:2). Then in Ephesians 5 we are told that husbands should love their wives just as the Lord loves the church (v. 25). These portions of the Word show us clearly that the bride of Christ is not a physical house but a living composition of the redeemed ones.

THE NEW JERUSALEM AS THE TABERNACLE OF GOD WITH THE TEMPLE

In Revelation, we are also told that the holy city, the New Jerusalem, is the tabernacle of God (21:3). To Christ, it is a bride; to God, it is a tabernacle. God's intention is not to have a tabernacle built with wood and gold or a temple built with wood and stones. God's intention is to have a temple built with His living children. We are told in the Scriptures that we are the household and the house of God (Eph. 2:19; 1 Tim. 3:15), and we are the living temple of God (1 Cor. 3:16; Eph. 2:21-22). On the one hand, we are the living bride to match

Christ, and on the other hand, we are the living house, the living temple, the living tabernacle, the living habitation, to meet God's need. We are the bride to satisfy Christ, and we are the tabernacle to give God rest.

As we have seen, the Old Testament is a record of the history of the tabernacle and the temple. The same is true of the New Testament. When the Lord Jesus was on this earth, He was the tabernacle of God (John 1:14) and His body was the temple of God, which was destroyed on the cross by the Jewish people but raised up by the Lord in His resurrection in an enlarged way (2:19-21). So, the church is the enlarged Body of Christ as the enlarged temple of God. Eventually, when we come to the ultimate conclusion of the entire Scriptures, we have a picture of the tabernacle and the temple. This city is the very ultimate tabernacle, with God in Christ Himself as the temple. Therefore, this picture is the conclusion of the history of the tabernacle and the temple. What is the ultimate expression, the ultimate consummation, of the tabernacle and the temple? It is the holy city, the New Jerusalem, which is a living composition of all the saints from the Old Testament time to the New Testament time, all the chosen ones, all the redeemed people. All the people saved by God in Christ through the Spirit are the members to be built up as a living corporate Body, a living corporate city, a living corporate container to contain God in Christ through the Spirit to express the Triune God.

I believe that at this point we are clear about what God is after today. He desires to have a group of people mingled with Christ, transformed into the image of Christ, and built up together as a corporate Body to contain Christ and express Christ. As we have seen before, at the beginning of the book of Revelation there are the seven lampstands as the local expressions of this Body, and at the end there is the New Jerusalem as the great, universal lampstand. It is the universal and ultimate consummation and completion of the church, having God as the light, Christ as the lamp, and the city as the stand to express God in Christ. This is the central thought of God, and this is the aim, the goal, and the direction of the work of God today.

CHAPTER TWELVE

THE TWO CORPORATE BUILDINGS—
BABYLON AND THE NEW JERUSALEM
AND
THE ASPECTS OF THE NEW JERUSALEM
(1)

Scripture Reading: Rev. 17:1-5; 21:9-10, 2-3, 22-23; 22:1-2;
S. S. 6:4

In this chapter I wish to show you a contrast, a comparison, between two cities, the mysterious Babylon and the holy New Jerusalem. As we pointed out in the previous chapter, the intention of God is to build up a corporate Body, a corporate vessel, with humans mingled with God Himself to contain God and express God. However, the enemy of God came in before God did to work himself into the human nature, so that humans have become the materials for Satan to build up an evil, sinful, corporate vessel to contain and express Satan instead of God. The whole history of the human race is a history of this evil, sinful, satanic building. From the time of Cain, the second generation of the human race, Satan began his building. He built a human society as a corporate vessel to contain himself and express all his sinful aspects.

In the Scriptures a city is a sign of the human community built up with humans as its materials. It is a sign of a living community, either of Satan to contain Satan or of the living Body of Christ to contain God. Today, the human community as a corporate vessel contains Satan with all his sinful aspects, and Satan is expressed through it. Whether in the Far East or in the West, whether in Europe or in Africa, all the human communities are parts of the satanic building as a corporate vessel to contain and express Satan. We can see Satan expressed, for example, in the night clubs and movie theaters in many places. After the fall of man, Satan utilized the human race as materials to build up human civilization as a vessel to contain him and to afford him a resting place, a habitation. Human civilization, the human community, is a satanic dwelling place, a resting place for Satan to have his satisfaction and rest.

JERUSALEM AND BABYLON IN THE OLD TESTAMENT

After the city of Babel and its tower were built to contain and express Satan, God chose Abraham from that region and brought him out to an elevated land, the land of Canaan, which represents the heavenly realm in resurrection. God's intention was to make Abraham a house and a kingdom with a people as the materials for God's divine building. However, the children of Israel were brought down to Egypt through the subtlety of the enemy Satan. Instead of building God's divine building, the children of Israel built cities for Pharaoh, the enemy of God. However, immediately after God delivered them out of Egypt, He commanded them to build a tabernacle. For forty years in the wilderness they were always for this building. Then, when they entered the land of Canaan, after they subdued all the enemies, they built a temple in the city of Jerusalem as a more solid habitation for God.

The city that Satan built up with the second race of humans was first called Babel and then Babylon. God chose a people as a new race to be another people, the heavenly people, to build up another city, that is, Jerusalem. The history of the Old Testament is a history of the fighting and struggling between these two cities, Babylon and Jerusalem. These two cities represent two corporate bodies, two corporate vessels. Babylon represents a satanic vessel, and Jerusalem represents a divine vessel. Babylon represents a civilization, a community, of the human race as a container to contain and express Satan, while Jerusalem represents a chosen people as a container to contain and express God. These two cities always opposed each other. Eventually, Babylon came to destroy Jerusalem with the temple and capture all the vessels in the temple for the worship of God, placing them in the temple of idols. Later on, when the people of Israel returned to Jerusalem, they brought all these vessels from Babylon back to Jerusalem to restore the worship of God in the temple and in the city. This is the history of the Old Testament.

JERUSALEM AND BABYLON IN THE NEW TESTAMENT

Now, let us see the history in the New Testament. The New Testament, as we have said before, is also a record of building. Immediately after we recognize that the Lord Jesus is the Christ, the Son of the living God, the Lord tells us that we are stones as the materials for His building of the church (Matt. 16:18). Building in the New Testament begins at this point. However, while God is building His church, Satan is also building his building. God is building the New Jerusalem, and Satan is building Babylon. Eventually, throughout all the Scriptures, there are these two cities, the New Jerusalem as the building of God and Babylon as the building of Satan.

We should not believe that Babylon is only a material city. Rather, Babylon is a sign, signifying people as a human community used by Satan as a corporate vessel to contain and express him. Likewise, we should not believe that the New Jerusalem is a heavenly mansion. The New Jerusalem is also a sign. It signifies all the chosen, redeemed people of God as materials built up together as a corporate vessel to contain God and express God. Therefore, in the whole universe, with the human race, there are two communities, the satanic community and the divine community. The satanic community is a corporate vessel to contain and express Satan, and the divine community is a corporate vessel to contain and express God.

I must reiterate these things because in Christianity there is a wrong concept concerning the New Jerusalem. In some places certain ones have come to me and said, "Brother Lee, you have taken away our heavenly mansion. Our only hope was to go to the heavenly mansion, but according to your teaching and interpretation, our heavenly mansion is gone."

Whether or not your heavenly mansion is gone is not up to me. My burden from the Lord is to help His children realize what the central thought and heart's desire of God is. Do you think that God is looking for a heavenly mansion with millions of rooms, one room for each believer? This thought is ridiculous; it is too childish. God is not looking for such a thing. Rather, God is looking for a community, a composition of living persons redeemed by Him, regenerated by Him, transformed by Him, and mingled with Him as a corporate vessel to contain Him in Christ and to express Him through Christ. This is God's desire, and this is the New Jerusalem.

This thought is not only in the New Testament; it is also in the Old Testament. One day the Lord revealed to me Song of Songs 6:4. This verse says, "You are as beautiful, my love, as Tirzah, / As lovely as Jerusalem." Here we see that the bride, the one who is seeking the Lord, is likened by the Lord to Jerusalem. So, the thought of Jerusalem being the bride of the Lord is clearly seen in both the Old and New Testaments. However, to see the vision of the New Jerusalem we need to be brought to a high mountain. The two visions in Revelation, the vision of Babylon and the vision of the New Jerusalem, are in contrast. In Revelation 17, the apostle John was carried away in spirit into a wilderness to see the vision of Babylon (v. 3). In order to see the vision of Babylon, there is no need to go to a high mountain; it is sufficient to be in the wilderness. However, for John to see the vision of the New Jerusalem, he had to be carried away onto a great and high mountain (21:10). If you want to see something heavenly, you have to be in the heavenly place. If you want to see something eternal, you have to be on the spiritual height, on the spiritual high place. If you remain in the wilderness, you can see only Babylon and can never see the New Jerusalem, the heavenly city. If you want to see the heavenly city, you have to be delivered from the wilderness to the height of the heavenly places.

GOD AS LIGHT IN THE NEW JERUSALEM

Now we must go further to see more details concerning this corporate heavenly vessel. With passages such as Revelation 21 and 22, we must be very much before the Lord, looking to Him for the proper understanding. Hence, when we come to the details of the New Jerusalem, we cannot go too fast. God in Christ is the center of the New Jerusalem as the divine vessel. We may also say that Christ as the expression of God is the center of this divine corporate vessel. In the picture of the New Jerusalem, the invisible God is likened to light that shines with glory (21:11, 23; 22:5). When light shines, it does a work. Light is a ruling power; it rules when it shines. Darkness, on the other hand, brings in confusion and disorderliness without any rule. In order to destroy a government, you must first throw everything in it into darkness. Similarly, when you turn off the lights in a room, everything is in confusion and disorder, but when you turn the lights on again, the light rules and brings everything back into order. If all the lights in a major city were to go out, the whole city would be in darkness, and there would be robbery, looting, and killing. When the lights come back on, however, there is the ruling and governing, and the entire city is restored to good order.

In the six days of God's creation for restoration, the first thing restored was the light (Gen. 1:3). When God divided the light from the darkness, light came in to rule (vv. 4, 16). Where God is, surely there is light shining, and where God shines, there is the ruling power. If we have the presence of God in the church, we have the light, we are in the light of God, we are in God as light, we are under the light of God, and all of us are ruled. All confusion is subdued, and all things are brought into order. If there is confusion among us, it simply means that we do not have God as light and that we are in darkness. Today the church is a miniature of the New Jerusalem. In this smaller New Jerusalem, if we have God as the center in Christ, we have the light, and the first thing light does is rule everything and keep everything in order. When light shines, it also generates. Life comes from light. When the light of God shines into you, the life of God comes into you. Light always brings life to us. When we have God as light, we first have order and then life. We can see this in Genesis 1. On the first day when light came in, there was the dividing; that is, the keeping of order began. Before light came in, everything was in chaos. After light came in, light was divided from darkness and things began to be kept in order. After this, the waters below were divided from the waters above, and life came out of this order. If there is the light of God, there is the ruling power and there is order, and if there is the ruling power and order, there is the generating power, the yielding of life. All kinds of lives came out because of the light. This is the picture in the New Jerusalem. God is the ruling center of the New Jerusalem as the shining light. From this light come out all the riches of life. God is light and from Him flows the river of water of life, and in this living water grows the tree of life.

GOD AS LIGHT BEING
IN CHRIST THE LAMB AS THE LAMP

Furthermore, this very God, who as light rules and generates all the time, is in Christ the Lamb as the lamp. Revelation 21:23b tells us that the glory of God illumines the city, and its lamp is the Lamb. Just as light cannot be separated from a lamp, so God can never be separated from Christ. If light is separated from a lamp, the light is no more, and if the lamp is separated from the light, the lamp is no longer a lamp because it does not have light. Hence, light is one with the lamp. This picture shows us that God is one with Christ. God is the light and Christ as the Lamb is the lamp. They cannot be separated; they are two in one.

Moreover, as the Lamb, Christ is the redeeming One. Without Him as the redeeming One, we can never come to touch, to contact, God as light since we are so sinful and so much in darkness. Because no one can exist or stand before God in His light, we need redemption; we need the Lamb. It is only by redemption and by the blood that we can come to contact God. First John chapter one says that God is light and that when we come to fellowship with Him, we are in the light (vv. 5, 7a). Then when we are in the light, we see how sinful we are, so we need the blood of Jesus to cleanse us (v. 7b). When we are in the light of God, we need redemption; that is, we need the Lamb. We can testify this from our experience. Whenever we contact God as light, we have the sense that we need redemption, we need the redeeming blood of the Lord, and we need the Lord as the Lamb. Christ as the Lamb, the redeeming One, is the Mediator between God and man (1 Tim. 2:5). Through Him and in Him we can contact God, and in Him and through Him God can reveal Himself to us. Today God, who is light, is in the Lamb, the redeeming One, and in eternity Christ will still be the Lamb in whom the very God who is light will be experienced by us. Furthermore, the Lamb, who is the redeeming Christ, is the very expression of God, who is light.

GOD AS LIGHT IN THE REDEEMING CHRIST EXERCISING HIS AUTHORITY

God is in Christ, Christ is the expression of God, and God in Christ is on the throne at the center of the New Jerusalem (Rev. 22:1). These three items—God as light, the redemption of Christ, and the authority in the light—are a picture of the authority, the headship, and the lordship of God in Christ.

According to the measurements of the holy city, the New Jerusalem is a mountain. The city itself lies square, and its length, breadth, and height are all twelve thousand stadia (21:16). The wall is one hundred and forty-four cubits high and is much lower than the city itself. This indicates that although the bottom part of the city is a square, the top part of the city must not be. Rather, the top of the city is a peak. Therefore, the city must be a mountain. The throne of God in Christ, no doubt, is on the top of the mountain. So, the throne is the highest and central point of the city. Everything comes out of this throne. The river flows from the throne in the midst of the street, which starts from the throne. Since this one street meets the need at all the twelve gates, it must start from the top where the throne is and spiral through the entire city to reach all the twelve gates.

This picture is very meaningful. God as light is in Christ as the redeeming One, and the throne of God in Christ is the exercise of His authority. Out of these three—light, redemption, and authority—come all things. If we have God as light in the redeeming Christ to exercise His authority among us today in the church, then we have everything. We have the tree of life, we have the river flowing with the living water, we have the street of life, and we have the golden city, the pearls as the gates, and the precious stones as the foundations. We have everything. All the aspects of the church and all the riches of the church come out of God as light in the redeeming Christ exercising His authority.

What we need today is to acknowledge the redemption of Christ, be under the light of God, and be in subjection to the authority of God. Sinners need to repent because the kingdom has come; this means that the authority of God, the divine heavenly ruling, has come. The kingdom of the heavens simply indicates the heavenly ruling. Why do we commit sins and constantly do things against God? It is simply because we do not subject ourselves under His authority. If we are willing to be subjected under His authority, everything is all right, and there are no problems. The divine authority is exercised in the light of God and in the redemption of Christ. Therefore, we have to receive the redemption of Christ that we may be in the light of God, and then we will be under the authority of God. Today in the church there is the need for God to exercise His authority as light in the redeeming Savior, Christ, and there is also the need for us to be subjected under His authority. When we realize the authority of God by the light of God in the redemption of Christ, we will have the riches of Christ. All the riches of Christ will be the reality in the church. Then we will have the real expression of Christ. The way to realize the real church life is to realize the redemption of Christ in the light of God and to subject ourselves to the authority of God, that is, to have God as light in the redeeming Christ exercising His authority over us. This is the only way for us to have the real church life.

CHAPTER THIRTEEN

THE ASPECTS OF THE NEW JERUSALEM
(2)

Scripture Reading: Rev. 21:2-3, 18, 21-22; 22:1-2

According to the divine thought in all the Scriptures, God always sees His redeemed ones as His wife and He Himself as the Husband. Hosea 2:16 says, "And in that day, declares Jehovah, / You will call Me My Husband / And will no longer call Me Baali [meaning, my Master]." God wanted His people, the children of Israel, to call Him Husband and to no longer call Him Master. In verse 19 He goes on to say, "And I will betroth you to Myself forever; / Indeed I will betroth you to Myself / In righteousness and justice / And in lovingkindness and compassions." Hence, it is clear that in the thought of God, the people of Israel were a wife to Him. The same divine thought is also revealed in Isaiah. God told the children of Israel that He as their Maker was their Husband and they were a wife to Him, and that for a small moment He had forsaken them, yet He would gather them and receive them back (Isa. 54:5-7). Not only so, in the book of Jeremiah God likens His people to a wife (3:1). We also very much appreciate the Old Testament book of Song of Songs. This book likens the Lord's seeking one to a bride who is beautiful in His eyes, and it likens the Lord Himself to the Bridegroom.

Then, in the New Testament, John the Baptist testified that the Lord is the Lamb of God (John 1:29), and he also testified that the Lord is the Bridegroom who has the bride (3:29). We need to ask who this bride is. The answer is found in the last book written by the same author, the apostle John. In the book of Revelation, John tells us clearly who and what the bride of Christ is; the bride is the New Jerusalem (21:9).

In this record we are told clearly that the One who marries this bride is called the Lamb. He is the Lamb as well as the Bridegroom. All the students of the Scriptures admit that the bride mentioned in John chapter three is a corporate bride composed of living persons, not a physical entity. Therefore, how can the bride in the last book written by the same author be a physical place? We have to admit that this city, the New Jerusalem, is the very bride whom the apostle John mentions in his Gospel, in John 3:29. Not only so, the apostle Paul tells us in 2 Corinthians 11:2 that he betrothed us, the believers, as pure virgins to one Husband, Christ.

On the one hand, as to the relationship between us and the Father, we are all males. Even the sisters are brothers. Second Corinthians 6:18 is the only instance in which the New Testament indicates that God has daughters. For the most part it tells us that the believers are sons of God. Christ does not have sisters but brothers; He is the Firstborn among many brothers (Rom. 8:29), not among many brothers and sisters. On the other hand, as to the relationship between us and Christ, we all are females. Even the brothers are females. We all are virgins betrothed to Christ. We are the bride of Christ and the wife of the Lamb. This thought is seen throughout the Scriptures. Eventually, when we come to the end of the Scriptures, we have a full picture of this divine thought. All the redeemed people of God throughout all the ages are composed together as a living city to be indwelt by God, that is, to be filled with God. All the redeemed people are the bride of the Lamb and the habitation of God. This is the proper meaning of the New Jerusalem.

Throughout the Scriptures there is the divine thought that the redeemed people of God are composed together to be a bride for Christ and a habitation for God. This is the ultimate conclusion of all the Scriptures and the ultimate expression of the thought of the Scriptures. The divine thought is that God desires to have a group of living persons composed together as a corporate Body to contain Him and to express Him in Christ through the Holy Spirit. This is the central thought of God and this is the very pattern of the church. In these days, we speak a great deal concerning the building up of the church and concerning the practice of the church life. We have to realize that the New Jerusalem is the unique pattern in the holy Scriptures concerning the church, the building up of the church, and the church life. If we want to know what the church life is and what the right way is for the building up of the church, we have to know the New Jerusalem. This is the very vision by which we are able to know what is the right way for the building up of the church and what is the real condition, the real situation, of the real church life.

THE LORD GOD THE ALMIGHTY AND THE LAMB AS THE TEMPLE

In the preceding chapter we saw the first three aspects of the New Jerusalem. First, God is light in this corporate vessel. Second, God as the light is in the lamp, that is, in the redeeming Christ as the Lamb. Third, this God as the light in the redeeming Christ is on the throne. So, we have the light, the redemption, and the authority. These are the first three items of the church life for the building up of the church. Now we come to the fourth item. In this city, God Himself in Christ is the temple. A temple is a building for people to worship and serve God. We have to realize that in the church, not only the One whom we worship is God Himself, but even the place, the environment, the building, in which we worship God must also be God Himself. Simply speaking, we have to worship God in God Himself. We do not worship God in a physical building. The physical place in which we are is not our temple. God Himself is our temple, and we worship God in God Himself. We enjoy the full presence of God. The presence of God is so practical, so full, and so rich that He even becomes the very atmosphere, the very environment, through which and in which we worship Him. This experience is in the church. We do not have a physical temple in which we worship God. The temple is God Himself, since in the New Testament time, everything positive is God Himself in Christ through the Holy Spirit. We do not worship as the angels do. The angels worship a God who is objective to them, who has nothing to do with them subjectively. However, we Christians worship a very subjective God. While we are worshipping

Him, He is in us and we are in Him. He is the One whom we worship, and He is the temple in which we worship Him. Everything is God Himself in Christ through the Spirit.

When you are going to offer a prayer to the Lord, that prayer must be something out of the Lord, something in the Lord, something with the Lord, and something as a part of the Lord Himself. Your prayer must not be something merely to the Lord or for the Lord. Likewise, when you are going to advise a brother about a certain matter, you should not advise him for the Lord, but you must advise him with something out of the Lord, within the Lord, and even as part of the Lord. This is what it means to have the Lord Himself as the temple in which we worship Him, and this is the meaning of the New Testament service. The New Testament service is subjective to such an extent that in it we and the Lord, the two, are mingled as one. The worshipper is one with the One who is worshipped. We pray to the Lord in the Lord. We minister to others in the Lord. We praise the Lord in the Lord. This is the correct meaning of having God as the temple. The temple is simply the presence of God.

Today Christians speak much about light, life, power, strength, and other matters. However, all these things are nothing but the Lord Himself. If we are in the presence of the Lord, we have life. If we are in the presence of the Lord, we have light. If we are in the presence of the Lord, we have power, strength, and authority. If we are in the presence of the Lord, we have everything. God Himself in Christ through the Spirit is everything to us. More than twenty years ago we often preached the gospel on the street in the evenings. While one brother stood up to speak a word concerning the Lord Jesus, all the rest kneeled down to pray. At that time, none of us felt that we were on the street. Rather, we all felt that we were not only in heaven but also in the Lord. The Lord is the temple for our service of gospel preaching.

THE ENTIRE CITY BEING GOLD

The fifth aspect of the New Jerusalem is that the whole city itself is gold. In all the Scriptures, gold signifies the divine nature, the nature of God the Father. The city itself is pure gold without any mixture (Rev. 21:18b). This indicates that the church must be one hundred percent of God; it must be absolutely of the divine nature. Today among Christians, however, the church is a mixture with some part of the divine nature and some part of the fallen human nature. If we want to have the real church life, the church herself must be pure gold, that is, altogether of the divine nature. Here we need the work of the cross to purify us and to purge us.

About thirty years ago, I heard a short word saying that being pure is different from being clean. When I first heard that word, I could not understand it, and I was very surprised. I thought that to be cleansed was good enough. However, the speaker said that we still need to be purified, just as pure gold is purified to contain no mixture and to be transparent. Since that time the Lord has gradually shown me the difference between being clean and being pure. A dear brother may be nice, gentle, and clean but still have a mixture. He is not transparent but opaque. He is nice and clean, but you cannot see through him. When I am surrounded by brothers who have a mixture, I say, "Lord, deliver me. I am in a 'prison cell,' and every side is opaque." The more such brothers talk, the more they are in darkness, even if they are clean persons. To be clean is one thing, but to be pure and transparent is another. Sometimes you may meet a saint in the Lord, whom you sense is not only clean but also transparent, like clear glass. I had a history with Brother Watchman Nee for over thirty years. Within all those years, every time I met him I had the sense that he was a transparent man. When I sat before him, I could see through him. Every time he stood on the platform to give a message, the audience could sense that he was transparent. When he opened his mouth to speak only a few words, you could sense that everything became transparent. Brothers and sisters, we should be clear that simply to be clean is not enough. We need to be purified by the death of the Lord on the cross.

THE RIVER OF WATER OF LIFE PROCEEDING OUT OF THE THRONE OF GOD AND OF THE LAMB

The sixth item we need to consider concerning the New Jerusalem is the river of water of life proceeding out of the throne of God and of the Lamb (22:1). When we have God as light in the redemption of the redeeming One, Christ, and when we are under the authority and recognize the headship and lordship of Christ, and when we experience the divine nature among us, there is always a flow of life, a living stream, flowing among us. This flowing of the living water is the fellowship of the entire city, and it is the source, the fountain, the well, of the supply for the entire city. Where the flow of the river reaches, there the supply is ministered. This flow of the living stream comes out of the lordship and the headship realized by us in the redemption of Christ with the light of God. If we give up the headship of the Lord in the church and do not recognize the divine authority, there is no possibility for us to have the living stream flowing among us all the time. Suppose that we as a group of believers come together to realize the oneness of the Body of Christ and try to have the church life, yet whenever we come together, every one quarrels with one another. If so, do you believe there is the possibility of having the living stream flowing among us? There is no possibility. As long as the throne of God is gone, the source of the living water is also gone, because the living water comes out of the throne of God. As long as you do not have the headship, the lordship, of Christ realized in the divine order, you have lost the source of the living water. If we realize the lordship, the headship, of Christ in the divine authority in the redemption of the redeeming One and in the light of God, the river of living water constantly flows to bring the life supply to us.

What is this river of living water? No doubt, it is a symbol of the Holy Spirit. John 7:37-39 confirms this. In verse 38 the Lord told us that he who believes into Him, as the Scripture said, out of his innermost being shall flow rivers of living water. Then verse 39 says, "This He said concerning the Spirit." The Holy Spirit whom the Lord ministers to us is a flowing river of water of life within us. Hence, in the picture of the New Jerusalem there is God the Father as the light, God the Son as the redeeming One, and God the Spirit as the flowing One. Light is with God the Father, redemption is with God the Son, and life is with God the Spirit. Therefore, He is called the Spirit of life (Rom. 8:2). God as life to us is always flowing. First, He flows out in the Son, and then He flows out as the Spirit. He is the light, He accomplished redemption in the Son, and He flows out as the Spirit to be the life supply. Here is the light, the lamp, and the river, and here is the Triune God. The light is the Father, the lamp is the Son, and the river is the Spirit. In the church life, if we realize the headship of Christ in the light by His redemption, we have the Spirit flowing all the time within us and among us as the life supply. This is a requirement for the church life. If we do not have this, we will be thirsty and dried up.

THE TREE OF LIFE GROWING
IN THE FLOW OF THE LIVING WATER

The seventh aspect of the New Jerusalem is that the tree of life grows in the flow of the living water (Rev. 22:2). This means that where the flowing of the living water is, there is the life supply. The tree of life is Christ as life and the life supply to us. That the tree of life grows in the river means that Christ as our life supply is available to us in the flow of the Spirit. If you have the Spirit, you have Christ as the tree of life, the life supply.

As the church, we must have the flow of the Spirit. In this flow of the Spirit we have the supply of Christ; that is, we have Christ as the supply. Merely to preach doctrines and teachings does not work. We must have Christ ministered to us as the life supply through the flow of the Spirit. Whenever we come together, there must be the flow of the stream, and in this flow of the stream there is the supply of Christ, Christ ministered to us as the life supply. Brothers and sisters, it is useless to argue about the way to meet. We need to check ourselves by asking, "Is our meeting full of Christ as the supply ministered to us?" This is a real test. In any kind of meeting of the church life, there must be Christ ministered as the life supply in the flowing stream of the Holy Spirit. Every kind of meeting must be checked concerning the ministering of Christ as the living supply.

In the church life, we must have Christ supplied and ministered to us as the life supply in the flow of the Holy

Spirit. Revelation 22:1-2 indicates the riches of the supply of Christ. There are twelve different kinds of fruit, fresh and rich. Christ is not limited or poor. He is unlimited and unsearchably rich (Eph. 3:8). We must always have something new and fresh of Christ to minister to His people. Even in our singing of hymns we must not be old or poor. Day by day, week by week, month after month, and year after year, we should not be satisfied with singing the same hymns over and over. Is Christ this poor? We need to try to write more new hymns to bring in the riches of Christ in the flow of the Holy Spirit. I have heard much singing of the Psalms, but I do not sense much supply of Christ in those Psalms. There are more riches of Christ in books such as Ephesians, Colossians, and Philippians. All these books contain the riches of Christ. In some of the Psalms we are told to shout and to cry aloud. However, we may give a poor shout, a poor cry, with nearly nothing of Christ. In the meetings we must have something of the riches of Christ ministered to the Lord's people as the life supply. We must bring Christ as the new fruits, as the fresh supply.

THE STREET OF THE CITY

The eighth aspect of the New Jerusalem is the street. With the flow of the river and with the growth of the tree of life, there is a street (Rev. 22:1-2). The street, the way, is Christ Himself, just as the tree of life is the Lord Himself. The Lord told us, "I am the way and the reality and the life" (John 14:6). With and in the flow of the living water grows the tree of life, and the flow of the living water is in the middle of the street. This means that if you have the street, you have the flow, and if you have the flow, you have the way.

Moreover, this way is pure gold, like transparent glass (Rev. 21:21). This is a picture which we have to understand figuratively. God as the light and Christ as the lamp are on the throne, and the flow of living water is the Holy Spirit. With the Holy Spirit is Christ as the tree of life, the life supply, and the flowing of the living water is on the street, the way, which is Christ Himself. In order to experience Christ as the street, you need to have the pure gold of the divine nature, you need to have the flow of the Holy Spirit, and you need to enjoy Christ as the life supply. If you do not have the pure gold with the flow of the living water and the tree of life growing in this water, there is no street, no way, to walk on. Many times brothers have come to me, saying, "Brother Lee, I don't know what I should do in this matter. I don't know what is the right way for me to take." My answer has always been, "Do you have Christ within you? Do you have the living stream within you? Do you enjoy Christ as the living One and the life supply? Then do not speak about the way; speak about Christ. If you have Christ as the pure gold, the living water, and the living supply, you have the way, and you will know what you should do." Once, a brother who was having trouble with his wife came to me, saying, "Brother Lee, according to the Scriptures, we should be a certain way, and according to the law of the Chinese government, we should be a certain way. Is this right or not?" I said, "Yes," but then I asked him, "Brother, since you have the Bible and you have the Chinese law, both of which are very clear, why do you come to me?" He said, "Even though I have the Bible and the Chinese law, I still don't know how to deal with my wife." Then I asked him, "You have the Bible, but do you have Christ within you? You have the Chinese law, but do you have the stream flowing within you? Have you enjoyed Christ today? Have you enjoyed Christ in this very trouble which you are having with your wife?" Brothers and sisters, test yourself with these three matters: Do you have Christ? Do you have the flowing stream? Have you experienced Christ in the particular matter which you are facing? By testing yourself in this way, you will know what you should do. The street, the way, is not in teachings or doctrines but in the living Christ, the living stream. If you have the stream, you have the life supply and you have the pure gold, the divine nature; that is, you have the street. Furthermore, the one street proceeds from the throne of God to meet the needs at each of the twelve gates. We believe that this street is a spiral, circling around all the time and reaching all the twelve gates. Therefore, once you get on the street, you can never be lost.

Remember well that if we are going to have the real church life, we must have God as light, and we must realize

the lordship, the headship, in the divine authority through
the redemption in God as light. Then we have the divine
nature, the flow of the living water, and the life supply, that
is, Christ Himself. Eventually, we have the living way. We
know how to do things, we know how to go on, and we know
how to walk to follow the Lord. Everything with us is clear,
pure, and transparent. Nothing is opaque, and no one is lost.
This is the way to have the church life.

CHAPTER FOURTEEN

THE ASPECTS OF THE NEW JERUSALEM
(3)

Scripture Reading: Rev. 21:2-3, 10-14, 16-19, 21-23; 22:1-2

We have seen that the New Jerusalem is a full picture of all the building work of God throughout the generations. It condenses all the thoughts, main points, and main lines of all the Scriptures. If we study the Scriptures carefully with the help of the Holy Spirit, we will be very clear that God's intention is to give Himself to us as life in Christ and through the Holy Spirit. In this way, God is able to mingle Himself with us and cause us to be built together as a corporate Body, a corporate vessel, a corporate container, to contain God in Christ through the Spirit and to express God through Christ. This is the central thought of God.

God is triune; God the Father is embodied in the Son, and the Son is realized as the Spirit. First, God flows out to be life to us in Christ. When Christ came, He told us that He is the bread of life which comes down out of heaven, the food of eternal life from heaven (John 6:47-51). Second, God flows out to be life to us by the Holy Spirit, who is the living water for us to drink (7:37-39). God first flowed out to us through the Lord Jesus as our food supply, and then He flowed Himself into us as the Holy Spirit to be the living water for us to drink. God the Father in the Son is food to us, and God the Father as the Spirit is drink, the living water, to us. Therefore, we can feed on the Lord Jesus and drink of the Holy Spirit. When we feed on the Lord Jesus and drink of the Holy Spirit, we enjoy the Triune God, we experience the Triune God, and we are mingled with the Triune God as one. In this very experience of this enjoyment of the Triune God, we are built up together as one corporate Body. On the one hand, this corporate Body is a bride for Christ, a counterpart to match Christ. On the other hand, this corporate Body is a habitation, a dwelling place, for God to be His satisfaction and rest. Eventually, when we come to the end of the Scriptures, we have the New Jerusalem as a picture, showing how God is everything to us, how He is life to us in Christ, how He is the living water to us in Christ through the Holy Spirit, how He by being life and everything to us is mingled with us, and how He builds us together as one corporate Body to contain Him in order to express Him. In the holy city, the New Jerusalem, God is everything in Christ through the Spirit.

The writer of Revelation, the apostle John, is the same as the writer of the Gospel of John. If you pay full attention to this matter, you will realize that all the things the apostle John spoke of concerning the Lord Jesus in his Gospel are condensed and embodied in the picture of the New Jerusalem. In his Gospel, John tells us that the Lord Jesus is the Lamb of God (1:29). He also tells us that the Lord Jesus is the Bridegroom who has the bride (3:29-30) and that He is the light (1:4; 8:12), the way, the reality, and the life (14:6). Then he tells us that the Lord Jesus is the living bread from heaven, full of the life supply, and the living water (6:51; 7:37). All these items are condensed and embodied in the picture of the New Jerusalem.

Furthermore, the picture depicted in the last two chapters of the entire Scriptures concerning the New Jerusalem corresponds to the picture portrayed in the first two chapters of the Scriptures. In the first two chapters of the Bible we see the tree of life, and we also see a river flowing by the tree of life. Then we see gold, bdellium (pearl), and precious stones in the flow of the river by the tree of life. Here there is the tree of life, the flow of the river, and three items of precious materials for the building. Now in the last two chapters of the Bible, again we see the tree of life, the river of water of life, and the gold, pearls, and precious stones as materials for the building.

There is a difference between the materials at the beginning of the Bible and the materials at the end of the Bible. In Genesis 2 the three precious items were merely materials;

they were not yet built. The materials were present, but there was not yet a building. However, when we come to the ultimate consummation, we see a building built with these three kinds of materials. The holy city, the New Jerusalem as the divine building, is built with gold, pearls, and precious stones. Whereas at the beginning of the Scriptures we have a garden, at the end of the Scriptures we have a city. A garden is a scene of nature, of God's creation; a city is something built up with the materials created by God. In the first two chapters of the Scriptures we see a beautiful scenery of God's creation centered on a garden. But at the end of the Scriptures we see a beautiful building as the ultimate conclusion of the building work of God throughout all the generations.

If you would ask me what God has been doing from Genesis 3 to Revelation 20, I will tell you that God has been doing only one thing, that is, the work of building. God is carrying out this work by building Himself with His chosen and redeemed people. God is the Creator, and all creation is the creature with humans as the center. Although He is the Creator, His intention is to build Himself into man as His creature to mingle Himself with him. He desires to be the contents of His creature and to make His creature a vessel to contain Him, the Creator. This is the very central thought of God, and this is the real meaning of the church. What is the church? The church is a composition of created human beings mingled with the Creator. The Creator, the Triune God, is the contents of this people, and this people is built up together as a corporate Body to contain God and express God in Christ through the Holy Spirit. Therefore, the church is a group of people who are regenerated by God, filled by God, occupied by God, transformed by God, and who contain God and express God all the time. This is the very meaning of the church. God in Christ through the Spirit is the contents of this corporate Body, and this corporate Body is the vessel to contain God and express God. The reason we must spend so much time on this picture of the New Jerusalem is that this is the only picture in all the Scriptures which fully shows us the real situation, the real condition, and the real nature of the church.

THE GATES OF THE CITY

In the previous chapters we have covered eight points concerning the New Jerusalem as a picture of the church. Now we come to the ninth point, the gates. A gate is an entrance, an opening, through which one can have a share with something inside a building. If we are going to have a share in this divine building, we have to enter through the gates. What are the gates? Revelation 21:21 says, "And the twelve gates were twelve pearls; each one of the gates was, respectively, of one pearl." The city itself is pure gold (v. 18), but the gates are pearls, each gate being of one pearl. In the types of the Scriptures, gold is something which is different, distinct, from all other things. It represents the holy nature of God, which is a nature of separation, a separating nature. What then is the meaning of the pearl? Pearls are produced by oysters. When an oyster is wounded by a grain of sand, it secretes its life-juice around the grain of sand and makes it into a precious pearl. This signifies how Christ as the living One came into the death water and was wounded by us on the cross. After we wounded Him, we stayed at His wound to receive what He accomplished on the cross and to receive the divine secretion of the divine life, the resurrection life. The resurrected Lord secretes His divine life-juice around us all the time until we, the worthless grains of sand, become the precious pearls. We were created as grains of sand, but we were regenerated as pearls. It is by regeneration that we obtain an entrance into the divine things. In John 3:5 the Lord told us, "Unless one is born of water and the Spirit, he cannot enter into the kingdom of God." Once we are regenerated, we have the entrance into the things in the divine realm. This means we have the gates of pearl.

The holy city, New Jerusalem, has twelve gates (Rev. 21:12, 21), with three gates on each of its four sides (v. 13). Three is the number representing the Triune God. That there are three gates on each side signifies that the three of the Triune God—the Father, the Son, and the Spirit—work together to bring people into the holy city. This is indicated in the three parables in Luke 15. In the first parable we have

God the Son finding the sinners as the shepherd looking for the lost sheep (vv. 4-7). In the second parable we have God the Spirit finding the sinners as the woman seeking her lost coin (vv. 8-10). And in the third parable we have God the Father receiving the repenting and returned sons as the father receiving his prodigal son (vv. 11-32). Thus, the three of the Triune God—God the Father, God the Son, and God the Spirit—work together to bring sinners back and to bring sinners in, in order to have a share of the divine things.

In Revelation 21, *four* represents the four directions of the earth—the east, the north, the south, and the west. The gates on the four sides facing the four directions of the earth signifies that the gospel is preached to all the directions of the inhabited earth and that the entrance into the holy city is available to all the peoples on earth. Furthermore, the number four signifies the creatures, because in Revelation 4:6 we are told that there are four living creatures around the throne of God. That there are three gates on each of the four sides, three times four being twelve, implies that the Triune God, the Creator, is mingled with man, the creature. The New Jerusalem is the mingling of God and man.

From which direction did you come in? I came in from the east, while many of you came in from the west. The brothers from South America and Africa can say that they came in from the south, and many Russians and Eskimos will say that they came in from the north. Praise the Lord that regardless of which direction you and I came in, we all came in through the gates; that is, we all came in through the same Triune God, through God the Father, God the Son, and God the Spirit. On every side, the three gates are the same. The directions are different, but the gates are the same. By the mercy of the Lord I have traveled to many places, to Japan, Southeast Asia, Europe, the Middle East, and Canada. When I was young, I thought that, as a Chinese believer, I would be different from the Japanese believers, the German believers, the American believers, and many others. Later on, however, I discovered that I was wrong. When I went to Japan, I met a group of Japanese believers who are exactly the same as I am. When I went to Southeast Asia, I met some Filipino believers and I found that they also are exactly the same as I am. Everywhere I went, whether Denmark, England, Italy, or the United States, I found that everyone who is a believer in Christ is the same as I am. Why is this? It is because we all came in through God the Father, God the Son, and God the Spirit. Because we all came in through the same Triune God, we all are the same. When I went to Japan, I could not speak Japanese, and they could not speak Chinese, yet we could speak by Christ with one another. I could say amen to them, and they could say hallelujah to me. When we knelt down to pray, we could pray together wonderfully. I could not understand what they prayed in Japanese, but I could say amen! They could not understand what I prayed in Chinese, but they could say amen! This shows that we all came through the same gates, the same Triune God.

Not only so, after you enter through the gates, no matter from which direction you enter, once you walk on the street, you will be one with all the others. There is only one street. When we come in, we are all one. Unlike Los Angeles which has many streets, the New Jerusalem has only one street, which spirals from the top, from the throne of God, to the bottom of the mountain to reach the twelve gates. Once we enter the gates, we are on the street and we are with all the others. We are one in Christ, and we are one in His Body. The street is the way with the flowing of the living water. What is the flowing of the living water? It is the fellowship of the Holy Spirit. There is only one way, one street, one flow, one stream, one Spirit, one fellowship, and one food with twelve varieties. Everything is one. We are one. This is wonderful! Regardless of how you label yourself, sooner or later, you will have to give up your label. You may label yourself as a Presbyterian, a Baptist, a Methodist, a Pentecostal, an Episcopalian, or another name, but there are no such names in the New Jerusalem. Therefore, you must drop the names. You have to realize that you are a member of the New Jerusalem and that you are one with all the members. We are one in Christ and one in His one Body. No matter how you denominate yourself as a denomination, if you do not give that up today, one day the Lord will tell you, "Child, give that up." We are one in Christ, not in doctrine. We are one in the way, in the life, in the flow of the stream in the Spirit, and in the fellowship of the Spirit.

In these days, I have had a great deal of fellowship with many saints. One thing I have stressed is that we should be general and not try to be special. Do not say, "I am a Presbyterian," "I am a Baptist," or, "I am a Spirit-filled Christian." Forget about these labels. Simply remember that you were a sinner and now you have been saved. You are a saved one; that is all. Do not consider yourself higher than others. Do not consider that you are spiritual and others are not, nor consider that you have seen the heavenly vision and others have not. Give up all these thoughts. Regardless of what you think of yourself, as long as you are within the gates, you are one with me and I am one with you. We are all one in the way, in the life, in the Spirit, in the flow, in the communion, in the fellowship of the Spirit. Today in Christianity there are too many streams. There is the Presbyterian stream, the Methodist stream, the Lutheran stream, and so forth. However, in the New Jerusalem, there is only one stream. We all drink of the one water, we all feed on the one food, and we all walk on the one street. Furthermore, we have only one direction, that is, the direction toward the throne of God. We have one peak and one goal. We are marching on toward the top, the peak, toward the throne of God in Christ.

THE WALL OF THE CITY

Now we come to the tenth aspect of the New Jerusalem, the wall of the city. We have seen that the city itself is pure gold (Rev. 21:18b), the first item of the materials of the city. We have also seen that the gates are pearls (v. 21a), the second item of the materials. Now we must see that the wall is built up with precious stones (vv. 18a, 19-20), the third item of the materials. The three kinds of materials are related to the three persons of the Triune God. The pure gold is related to God the Father as the divine nature; the pearls are related to God the Son, Christ, as the crucified One, the wounded One, in whom we are regenerated; and the precious stones are related to the work of the Holy Spirit. Here we have the nature of God the Father as the pure gold, and the crucifixion, the redemption, and the regeneration of Christ to make us pearls. Now we need to have the working of the Holy Spirit upon us to make us precious stones.

A precious stone is not an original item of creation. It is something created by God that is burned to become like charcoal. Then, after being burned, it has to be burned more intensely with great pressure until it becomes a precious stone. According to an article I once read, a one-inch-square piece of carbon, when pressed under a weight of 800,000 pounds and burned in a heat of five thousand degrees, will become a small fine diamond. This is an illustration of the working of the Holy Spirit. Originally, we are not pieces of stone but pieces of clay. We need to be burned and pressed. We may think that because we are regenerated and are seeking the Lord, the Lord should be very happy with us and should be good toward us by always giving us good and happy days. However, we know that often it is just the opposite. The more we love the Lord and seek the Lord, the more we are troubled. After hearing this word, perhaps you will be frightened and try to run away, but the Lord's hand is upon you. You cannot run away because you are in the divine hand. He is the Potter and you are the clay (Rom. 9:20-21). Therefore, how can you run away? If you are able to run away, then try to do so. If you can give up being a Christian, try to do so, and the sooner the better. However, our being Christians is up to Him and not up to us; it is something from heaven and not something of this earth. You cannot give up the Lord. I tried a number of times to give up being a Christian, but I simply could not make it. The more I tried to give up, the more I had to love the Lord.

I must tell you the truth: The more you seek to love the Lord, the more there will be pressure and burning. On a given day, pressure may come from almost every side. Your dear wife is a pressure, your dear children are a pressure, and your dear brothers and sisters are a pressure. Everything is a pressure, and everyone burns you. Everywhere you go there is a furnace. You are just like the dough in a cake mold, put into the oven by the Cook. However, do not be afraid. The Cook knows how hot the oven should be. Whether it should be low, medium low, medium, medium high, or high, the divine

Cook knows how to adjust the fire. He will "cook" you in the right way. He will press you, and He will burn you until you become a properly baked "cake," suitable to His taste. He will press you and burn you until you become a diamond, a piece of precious stone. This is the work of the Holy Spirit.

In these days, Christians pay too much attention to the gifts. If a young man who has graduated from a seminary, who is eloquent in speaking, smart in thinking, and can recite some Bible verses, stands up to deliver a sermon in a wonderful way, people will admire and praise him. Such a young man may have a gift, but nothing of him may have passed through pressure and burning. I can never forget the lesson, the help, given to me by the Lord through Brother Watchman Nee when I was young and had just come out to serve the Lord. One day he sat in the living room with me alone. He said, "Brother, you have to realize that serving the Lord is not merely by the gifts. It is by something else that is more necessary." I asked him, "What is that something?" He said, "O brother, it is hard for me to tell you. You have to pass through the furnace to be burned and pressed." Then he went on to use the potter as an illustration. A potter makes a number of vessels or containers out of clay. Then he paints some beautiful patterns on the various pieces. The containers look beautiful, but they cannot be touched. A little touch will ruin them. So, the potter has to put all these vessels of clay with the beautiful paintings into the furnace to be burned. After the burning, they become solid. Whatever is painted on them can no longer be removed; it has been burned and wrought into them. This illustration shows us that the Lord needs us to be "burned" vessels with something of Him wrought into us by the work of the Holy Spirit. This is different from the gifts, which often hurt, damage, destroy, and spoil us.

As we have seen, the wall of the holy city is built with precious materials pressed and burned by the divine hand. We have to realize that we may have the gold as the city itself and the pearls as the entrance to the city, but if we do not have the precious stones, we do not have the wall. What is the function of the wall? The wall is for separation, and it is also for protection and safety. In many churches, there may be the gold, and there may be the pearls as the entrance, but they do not have the wall. Likewise, many believers have the gold within them, and they have the entrance, but they do not have the wall. They have never been built up. They are "flat" and "horizontal"; they have no dimensions. It is as if every part of them is an entrance. There is no separation, no protection, and no safety. There is nothing of the Holy Spirit wrought into them for them to be built up as a wall. We must have something of the Holy Spirit burned, wrought, into us to make us precious stones that we may be built up as a separation, as a protection, as a safeguard, as a separating line, to separate what is holy from what is worldly.

Furthermore, Revelation 21:18a says, "And the building work of its wall was jasper." Jasper is the appearance of the revealed God, the expressed God (4:3). When God reveals Himself, He appears as jasper, shining, transparent, with the divine expression. The wall of the holy city has the appearance of God, expressing the image of God. How can this be? It is simply because the believers, after the pressing and the burning, have been conformed to the image of God. Today we may have certain brothers who are nice and good naturally. When you meet them, you do not sense the appearance of God, the expression of God, the image of God. However, perhaps after five years they may have gone through some troubles, trials, burning, and pressing. When you meet them again, they may still be good and nice, but they are different. You will sense with them that there is the appearance of God, the expression of God, the image of God. You will see the divine jasper in them because they have been burned and pressed in the hand of the Holy Spirit. They have the appearance of God, and this very appearance of God is the boundary line, the separating line, of the church, separating what is of the church from what is not of the church and separating what is holy from what is worldly. The more you are like God, the more you are separated from the world. The more you express God, the more you have the separating line.

Revelation 21:14 says, "And the wall of the city had twelve foundations, and on them the twelve names of the twelve apostles of the Lamb." The wall is built upon the foundations of the apostles of the Lamb. This means that the wall is built upon the Christ who is brought to us by the apostles. Who are the apostles of the Lamb? They are the bearers of Christ. They are the transformed transmitting agents of Christ. That the wall is built upon the apostles of the Lamb simply means that the wall is built upon the Christ who is brought to us through the apostles as the transmitting agents. The children of Israel are the entrances, but the apostles of the Lamb are the foundations because they have Christ, and they brought Christ to us. This is a picture of the church. The church is built upon nothing other than the Christ brought and taught to us by the apostles.

THE EXPRESSION OF GOD IN LIGHT, LIFE, AND GLORY

Now we come to the last item of this holy city. The entire city is an expression of God in light, in life, and in glory. Revelation 21:11 says, "Having the glory of God. Her light was like a most precious stone, like a jasper stone, as clear as crystal." Thus, the whole city is an expression of God. It is a vessel, a container, a corporate Body, a built-up city to express God. This again is a picture of the church.

In conclusion, we must realize what the New Jerusalem is. The New Jerusalem is a living composition of all the saved persons throughout all the generations from the Old Testament time to the end of the New Testament time. They have been regenerated. They have been transformed in nature and in form. They have been changed absolutely into the same condition, the same situation, and the same form as God. Moreover, they have been built up together as a corporate vessel, a corporate container, to contain God and to express God. Therefore, God in Christ through the Spirit is the contents of this city, and God is the glory expressed through this city. This is the picture of the church. If we are going to understand the church and realize the real church life, we have to see this picture and understand all the aspects of this picture. May the Lord bless us in this matter.